'Twelve to One'
V Fighter Command Aces
of the Pacific War

SERIES EDITOR: TONY HOLMES

OSPREY AIRCRAFT OF THE ACES® • 61

'Twelve to One' V Fighter Command Aces of the Pacific War

Compiled by Tony Holmes

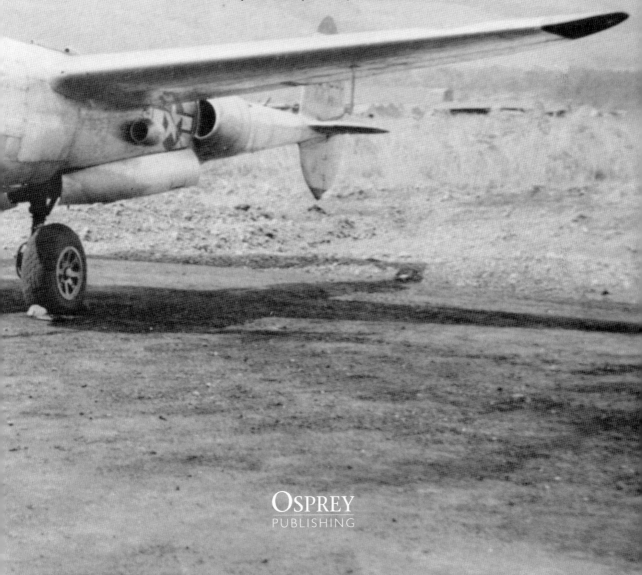

OSPREY
PUBLISHING

Front Cover

'On 2 November 1944, I was leading a squadron flight of 14 P-38s out of Tacloban airstrip on a dive-bombing strike against Japanese shipping in Ormoc Bay, on the west side of Leyte. Intelligence reported a concentration of troop transports, with destroyer and cruiser escorts, landing troops in the area.

'Our strategy was to take the first six aircraft across the bay at low level, drawing naval ack-ack. This would permit the remaining aircraft, carrying 500-lb bombs, to make their attacks with minimum opposition. Although reports of enemy aircraft in sizeable numbers came in, we went unmolested during the first portion of the attack, and one of our pilots got a direct hit with a 500-lb bomb on a troopship.

'About the time decoy flights were pulling up at the far end of the bay, and the dive-bombing runs were almost over, enemy aircraft were spotted in several directions by our pilots. One was sighted at "six o'clock" to me. I went into a tight climbing turn to meet the enemy head-on. Since my wingman stayed glued to me during the turn, the enemy pilot lost his enthusiasm and broke off into a climbing turn. My position was better now, and the chase continued.

'Gradually I gained on the Jap, climbing in the process to 16,000 ft. He was identifiable now as one of the new "Jack" fighters. He elected to enter a shallow dive, which against the P-38 was decidedly unwise. I needed full power for quite a while to catch him, but at 10,000 ft, and indicating 400 mph, he was right in front of me at point-blank range. Two short bursts produced no apparent effect, but on the third burst the Jap disintegrated with a violent blast. Flying debris thundered against my P-38. My windshield was smothered in Japanese engine oil. I had to use my side vision and the careful direction of my wingman to get back to base.

'During the disassembly of my P-38, a large portion of one of the pilot's maps was found in one of the oil cooler scoops. This momento is today a prized possession. Another momento of this combat is a copy of orders sending me Stateside from the Philippines after 22 months overseas. They are dated 1 November 1944. My most memorable mission had been unknowingly on my own time.'

This account, written by 14-kill ace Bob DeHaven, details the demise of his penultimate victory on 2 November 1944. Assigned to the 49th Fighter Group's 7th Fighter Squadron, DeHaven was, on this occasion, flying an unidentified P-38L that had almost certainly been commandeered from either the 8th or 475th FGs as an attrition replacement during the Philippines campaign. Seen here just seconds after flying through the fireball created by the exploding Mitsubishi J2M3 'Jack' fighter, DeHaven's P-38 is also featured in profile in the colour section of this volume (*Cover artwork by Mark Postlethwaite*)

First published in Great Britain in 2004 by Osprey Publishing, Midland House, West Way, Botley, Oxford OX2 0PH, UK
443 Park Avenue South, New York, NY 10016, USA

A CIP catalogue record for this book is available from the British Library

ISBN 978 1 84176 784 0

Edited by Tony Holmes
Page design by Mark Holt
Cover Artwork by Mark Postlethwaite
Aircraft Profiles by Chris Davey
Index by Alan Thatcher
Origination by PPS Grasmere Ltd. Leeds, UK
Printed and bound in China through Bookbuilders
Typeset in Adobe Garamond and Univers

08 09 10 11 12   11 10 9 8 7 6 5 4 3

ACKNOWLEDGEMENTS

The Editor wishes to thank both William Hess and John Stanaway for supplying the bulk of the photographs contained within this volume. Thank you also to Jim Doss for the provision of photographs and information relating to his late father, Col Edwin Doss. Lt Col Anthony Kupferer also generously lent photos of his wartime CO, Col Edward Roddy, for inclusion in this volume. Finally, thanks to 35th FG historian Carlos 'Dan' Dannacher, Jim Sterling and Carl Molesworth for the provision of photographs and information relating to pilots profiled in this book.

For details of all Osprey Publishing titles please contact us at:
NORTH AMERICA
Osprey Direct, C/o Random House Distribution Center, 400 Hahn Road, Westminster, MD 21157
E-mail: info@ospreydirect.com

ALL OTHER REGIONS
Osprey Direct UK, P.O. Box 140, Wellingborough, Northants, NN8 2FA, UK
E-mail: info@ospreydirect.co.uk
Or visit our website: www.ospreypublishing.com

CONTENTS

EDITOR'S INTRODUCTION

This volume is the third, and final, 'unofficial' war manual produced by the United States Army Air Force during World War 2. It followed similar books created by the Eighth Air Force's VIII Fighter Command in 1944, entitled *'Long Reach'* and *'Down to Earth'*, which served as 'bibles' for budding fighter pilots newly arrived in the European Theatre of Operations. Compiled by officers assigned to the staff of VIII Fighter Command, the text for these books was provided by both the leading aces and veteran fighter group leaders that were in the process of securing victory in the bloody skies over 'Fortress Europe'.

Almost certainly inspired by the production of VIII Fighter Command's *'Long Reach'* and *'Down to Earth'* manuals, the Fifth Air Force's V Fighter Command set about compiling its own report in the final months of the Pacific War. The task of producing the book was given to Col Roy R Brischetto, Assistant Chief of Staff of V Fighter Command's General Staff Corps. He duly set about contacting a number of the leading aces in-theatre, as well as several group commanders and a handful of lesser known, but no less experienced, frontline fighter pilots.

Some 26 airmen eventually submitted written reports for inclusion in the published document, which was titled *'Twelve to One'* to denote the kill ratio achieved by the fighter units assigned to V Fighter Command in World War 2. The booklet, subtitled *'Fighter Combat Tactics in the SWPA'* and clearly marked 'confidential' on its cover, was published on 1 August 1945. By then two of its contributors had been killed. The first to die was second-ranking American ace Maj Tom McGuire, who lost his life when his P-38 snap-rolled into the jungle and exploded when he tried to manoeuvre with a Ki-43 over Los Negros Island on 7 January 1945. Four months later the 35th FG's Maj 'Johnny' Young was killed in a freak accident at Clark Field, in the Philippines. One of his unit's P-51s lost a napalm tank on take-off, the store skidding across the runway until it hit Maj Young's jeep. Despite the pilot's best efforts to evade the tank, he received massive burns when it exploded upon impact with the jeep and died a week later. Finally, just five days after the publication of *'Twelve to One'*, ranking US ace Maj Dick Bong was killed when his P-80A jet suffered an engine flameout soon after taking off from Burbank, California.

Along with *Aircraft of the Aces 31 - VIII Fighter Command at War 'Long Reach'* and *Aircraft of the Aces 51 - 'Down to Earth' Strafing Aces of the Eighth Air Force*, this volume serves as a tribute to the memory of these brave men.

Tony Holmes
Sevenoaks
December 2003

PERIOD PREFACES

Brigadier General PAUL B WURTSMITH
US Army Air Force

This report is presented by V Fighter Command combat pilots for the purpose of making available helpful hints for combat replacement pilots who are assigned to duty in the Southwest Pacific Theater. This pamphlet is not intended to be a text devoted to air tactics, and the reader must bear that in mind.

The report is written by the combat pilots as they see air combat against the Japanese. These pilots include men who have logged an average of 500 combat hours or more, and list among their numbers Bong, Johnson, MacDonald, McGuire, Kearby, Lynch and many others of the team. Their record – over 2500 confirmed victories.

Credit for their success is shared in a large part by the men working on the line and in the various departments who are a major part of any flying team. It has been found by experience in this theatre that three rules must be followed by all fighter pilots who wish to be successful:

1. Never be surprised.
2. Always fight aggressively in pairs.
3. Never circle combat.

PAUL B WURTSMITH
Brigadier General

Brig Gen Paul 'Squeeze' Wurtsmith (left) poses with 475th FG Lt Col Charles MacDonald, and the latter's famous P-38J-15 42-104024, at Hollandia in the spring of 1944. Head of V Fighter Command from late 1942 until relieved by Brig Gen Freddie Smith in March 1945, Wurtsmith was a career aviator who had enlisted in the Army in 1928 and earned his wings four years later. Given command of the P-40C-equipped 49th Pursuit Group five days after the attack on Pearl Harbor, he had led the group into action in the defence of Australia in early 1942. Despite being promoted 'upstairs' to Fifth Air Force HQ, Wurtsmith would periodically sneak off in his personal P-38 in order to perform combat sorties with the '49ers'. Such flying earned him the unswerving devotion of his pilots. Awarded a second star, and promoted to major general, Wurtsmith was made commander of the Thirteenth Air Force on 1 March 1945. He was subsequently killed in a peacetime flying accident (*via William Hess*)

Brig Gen Freddie Smith replaced Maj Gen Wurtsmith as Commanding General of V Fighter Command on 1 March 1945. Smith, the former Chief of Staff to Fifth Air Force CO Gen George C Kenney, returned to the Southwest Pacific following a year of attached duty in the Pentagon with the USAAF Chief of Staff. He was well liked by the veteran fighter pilots who now occupied the various staff positions within the Fifth Air Force, and his inheritance of V Fighter Command from Wurtsmith had long been expected (*via William Hess*)

Brigadier General FREDERICK H SMITH JR
Commanding General V Fighter Command

This combat report of the V Fighter Command is an outgrowth of the hard and often bloody lessons which have been learned by fighter pilots and fighter units in this theatre since the early days at Darwin and Port Moresby. The men who have contributed to the text are those who have been through those difficult situations and conditions which are inherent in the Southwest Pacific Area. Their constant and aggressive teamwork have accomplished a rate of attrition against the enemy in excess of 12-to-1.

Similar texts published in the European theatre of operation have outlined battle conditions and situations there. It is hoped that readers of the V Fighter Command report will be able to visualise, and thus arm themselves against the probable enemy counters to our operations, and through lessons learned in the bitter engagements which have gone before, to enhance chances of victories and survival.

FREDERICK H SMITH JR
Brigadier General, Commanding
V Fighter Command
August 1945

8th FIGHTER GROUP

COL EARL H DUNHAM
COMMANDING OFFICER
8th FG

In considering the tactics employed by this unit, I would like to divide them into two general types. Those employed against aerial targets, and those employed against ground targets. In either type the outstanding criterion of success is leadership.

When planning a mission, it is impossible to go into too much detail. Briefing of pilots by intelligence and operations officers should be very thorough so as to leave no doubt in the mind of any pilot as to what the mission calls for, and what his specific job will be throughout the mission. As a good football player must eat, sleep and live football, thinking how he can best improve his playing, so must the combat pilot eats sleep, and live his flying tactics,

The formation that we use is the conventional two-ship element, with four aeroplanes in a flight. It is desired that our wingmen will be well up forward, with enough interval to the side so as not to hamper the manoeuvrability of the element, and yet close enough so that the two aeroplanes can offer mutual protection. This holds true also with the elements and flights. In group flights, the squadrons should be within visual distance of the leader. A four-aeroplane flight is the smallest desired unit when engaged in aerial combat with the enemy. When over the target, where ack-ack and interception are likely and a lot of turning or weaving is done, the squadron will usually end up with the elements in a string formation.

Long-range escort has gained ever increasing importance in the last few months, and this importance will continue to grow. Knowing your aeroplane is essential in any form of aerial combat, but this knowledge becomes increasingly important in long-range escort. Rendezvous must be made close to the target area, since the most economical speed for fighters is much faster than that of the escorted bombers. Because of the limited time over targets, when enemy opposition is expected, we like to send a small force in high so as to attack any enemy formation. This causes them to break up into small units which can then be easily taken care of by the main body of escorting fighters. This group of aeroplanes should be about five minutes ahead of the main striking force. While en route to the target on long missions, fuel is used from one belly tank at a time, and the empty tank is jettisoned, which cuts down on the amount of drag.

Attacks on ground or surface targets by dive-bombing are made either individually or by four-ship flights, depending on the nature and size of the target. When strafing, individual passes are never made unless no ack-ack is encountered. Four-ship flights are generally used, with all ships nearly line abreast. However, if the size of the target permits, more flights

The 8th FG's trio of squadrons (35th, 36th and 80th FSs) operated a number of fighters during their time in the Pacific, before finally settling on the P-38 in the spring of 1944. P-39s, P-400s, P-40s and P-47s were all flown in combat by the 8th, with the latter fighter replacing the Airacobras of the 36th FS during October-November 1943. This particular machine, P-47D-3 42-22604, was assigned to the squadron's 1Lt William 'Kenny' Giroux upon its arrival in Port Moresby in late October. Marked with a 'winged G', the machine was used by Giroux to probably destroy three Ki-21 'Sally' bombers north of Nadzab on the morning of 7 November. These were his only claims in the P-47, and this shot shows Giroux's fighter optimistically bearing two victory decals. Note the distinctive flat 200-gallon 'Brisbane' tank fitted to the fighter's centreline pylon, this store solving the range problems initially associated with the Thunderbolt in the Southwest Pacific. The tank's name was derived from its place of invention – the capital city of Queensland, Australia (*via John Stanaway*)

are brought up on line. Every advantage should be taken of the sun and clouds for use as elements of surprise. However, it should be remembered that the Japanese can use the same tactics, and frequently do.

In closing, I wish to state that the best offensive is in keeping together and hitting hard. Also, the best defence is obtained through the same procedure. A fighter pilot is an individual, and his thoughts and actions must be complete and instantaneous. Only unusually gifted persons must be singled out to lead, and as leaders they must strive for perfection. It is only through experience that this perfection can be obtained.

CAPT WILLIAM K GIROUX 36th FS/8th FG

Our tactics are very simple, and though we have had little chance to prove them, they worked out very well in the fights we had from 2 to 15 November 1944. During this period we shot down 32 enemy aeroplanes for the loss of only one P-38 and no pilots. At the time, only four members of the squadron had seen previous aerial combat, but during November we ran into almost every possible situation.

In some fights the enemy had every possible advantage, such as altitude (which is the best advantage they could ever hope to have), they fought over their own airfields, which gives their pilots a feeling of safety, and they had clouds in which to hide. Many times they outnumbered us. On other days we met them at equal altitude, and on occasions we sat above their strips watching them as they took off – but in every case we were the winners.

William K Giroux

William K 'Kenny' Giroux was born on 15 November 1914 in Chicago, Illinois, although he was raised on a farm in nearby Momence. Following graduation from high school in 1932, he worked at various occupations during the Depression, prior to joining the Army Reserves in the wake of the Pearl Harbor attack. When it came time for 'Kenny' to enter service, contrary to popular practice, he had to lower his age rather than raise it in order to qualify for flight training! He accomplished this, and graduated with Class 43-B at Luke Field, Arizona, on 6 February 1943.

Giroux was initially assigned to the Panama Canal Zone, where he flew P-39s with the 37th FG's 30th and 22nd FSs. Transferring to V Fighter Command in August 1943, he was assigned to the Port Moresby-based 36th FS/8th FG the following month. Issued with a P-47D-3, 'Kenny' first saw combat on 5 November 1943 when his unit intercepted a large formation of Ki-21 'Sally' bombers north of Nadzab. While his attacks were apparently successful, he had to settle for three bombers probably destroyed, as their final demise could not be confirmed. Shortly afterwards, his squadron was equipped with P-38s, and it was in a Lightning that he destroyed his first two victories – an A6M 'Zeke' on 15 March and a Ki-43 'Oscar' on 27 July 1944.

Giroux would have to wait until the invasion of Leyte for his next successes, the future ace downing three A6M 'Hamps' during a B-24 escort mission on 2 November. Now a regular flight leader, he 'made ace' just 48 hours later whilst on yet another escort mission, destroying three 'Oscars' over Alicante airfield. 'Kenny's' ninth kill – a Ki 61 'Tony' – came on 6 November, and his final aerial victory – yet another 'Oscar' – was claimed nine days later. Post-war, Giroux stated that his tally of ten victories was not really his total score, for he lost another three kills on the 'cut of the cards'. V Fighter Command did not permit the sharing of victories!

Giroux was forced to bale out of his mechanically-crippled P-38 on Christmas night 1944 whilst en route to Leyte, the ace discovering that the coolant shutters on the Lightning's right engine had seized – this may have been caused by Japanese anti-aircraft fire. He managed to coax his terminally ill fighter to San Jose island, where he baled out and swam ashore. Evading capture by the Japanese, Giroux eventually managed to locate American forces. Deemed tour-expired after this escapade, he returned home in February 1945.

Maj William K Giroux left the service post-war and enjoyed great success as a businessman in Kankakee, Illinois, until his retirement. He passed away at the Illinois Veterans' Home in Manteno on 1 September 1993.

'Kenny' Giroux poses for a semi-formal portrait, his A-2 flying jacket adorned with a 36th FS 'Flying Fiend' patch (*via John Stanaway*)

We had drilled into our pilots the advantage of fighting as a team, which usually meant that we split up into two-ship elements. We stressed that anybody can shoot down an aeroplane if he gets in range. We told the pilots, 'Hold your fire until you are sure of your aim – sure that the bullets will hit the target. You are lucky if you get a second shot at an aeroplane more manoeuvrable than your own. Aim to hit his gas tank, and a one-second burst will bring him down in flames'. The vital importance of keeping a two-ship element was pointed out again and again.

Sighting the enemy first almost always gives you an advantage. If he is above you, start climbing away from him – not at 180 degrees to his course, but out to the side where you can watch him. Keep a constant lookout to make sure that it is not a trap to draw your attention so another enemy aeroplane can attack you from the rear. Use a fast climb with an airspeed of better than 200 mph. If he dives on you, make a head-on pass. You have more firepower, and the chances are you are a better shot. After your pass, pull a tight turn, which forces him to turn and kills off the speed advantage he gained in the dive. A 270-degree turn should do it. Then climb away until you are far enough apart to turn back and attack in the way that best fits the circumstances.

Always maintain plenty of speed in a fight, then if you should miss a shot you can pull up for another pass. Never try to turn more than 90 degrees with any enemy aeroplane, or you will lose your speed. If you have a sunny day, use the sun to your advantage. It is one of the best places to hide. The Japanese seldom try to keep their altitude advantage. Although a fight may start at 20,000 ft, it will invariably end up on the deck, which is as good a place as any. They seem to have poor judgement in the turns at low level. On two different occasions I have seen them hook a wing in the trees or water as they were turning. One of their

'Kenny' Giroux is seen with his P-38J-15 at Owi, in the Schouten Islands, in September 1944. This aircraft carried the names *WHILMA II* (left) and *Dead Eye Daisy* (right) on either side of its nose, and its propeller spinners were painted white overall, with two black bands. A colour profile of this machine appears on page 65 (*via John Stanaway*)

favourite tricks is a 'split-S' when you get near them, and they have at least 2000 ft altitude. You can't 'split-S' with an enemy fighter, but turn so you can watch him while he performs his manoeuvres. Make another pass when he straightens out.

When flying in formation, enemy pilots get flustered under attack and usually split up, so if you are on one you have to watch carefully for other enemy aeroplanes. If ever you are caught from the rear, use a scissors manoeuvre with your wingman. Whichever aeroplane the Japanese fighter attacks should turn very sharply, allowing the other aircraft to get a shot at the enemy. Always shoot, even though you are out of range, when the enemy is on the tail of one of your aeroplanes. A few tracers may scare him off. Never be too proud to run for home or pull out of a fight if things are not going your way. Always stay in pairs and never get out alone. If you lose your wingman, or he loses you, join up with the nearest friendly aeroplane. Keep in a weaving string so that you can cover the blind spot on your wingman, and he can cover yours.

All new pilots should be briefed in the advantages we have over the enemy and the advantages he has over us. There are speeds and altitudes at which our aeroplanes can out-turn theirs. Most of our ships will out-climb and out-dive theirs. Know the limitations of your ship and of the enemy's ship.

Complicated tactics will work, but it would take months of practice for which we haven't time. Our wingmen are, for the most part, men with about 300 hours of flying time, and some have as low as 20 hours in fighter aircraft when they take off on their first combat mission. A programme of complicated tactics with pilots of so little experience would be useless.

I have not said anything about strafing and dive-bombing as yet, but in reality I think it is as important, if not more so, than aerial combat.

Like the P-38 seen opposite, the exact identity of this machine remains unclear. It is almost certainly not the same Lightning photographed at Owi, as the *Dead Eye Daisy* script has been applied in a different style of lettering. The dog motif on the nose is similar in style to the animal featured on the Owi P-38, but the latter did not feature a 36th FS 'Flying Fiend' emblem. Finally, the canine on the engine cowling is significantly different in style to the one that adorned the Owi Lightning. The name *Elmer* is also a new addition
(*via John Stanaway*)

A fighter pilot serving his tour of duty in this theatre will be very lucky if he is in more than half a dozen fights, but he will be required to do a great deal of dive-bombing and strafing. His targets will be shipping, airfields, trains, highway traffic, gun emplacements, camp areas, etc. These missions as a whole are far more dangerous than aerial combat, but with correct training and briefing, they can be made fairly safe. Pilots should study maps and photos of the areas they are to attack.

Again they should fire only when within range, and endeavour to destroy the target in one pass. The pass must be fast and the breakaway low. The pilot should stay on the deck until out of range of the ground fire. He must know the limitations of the ship so as not to mush into the ground. Care should be taken not to get so intent on the target that the pull-out comes too late. Dive-bombing with fighters is accurate, and our aeroplanes are very hard targets for their anti-aircraft fire. After releasing his bombs, the pilot should break away and hit the deck.

To sum it up, combat flying can be made almost as safe as an OTU if the replacement pilots are FIGHTER PILOTS, and properly trained before they enter the squadron. Being well briefed before and after each mission is also a very important item.

The kind of replacement pilot we like is one who has trained in fighters because he knows it is the best flying training in the field of aviation, one who knows his ship well enough to respect it, but not fear it, one who has had at least 50 hours of gunnery, both aerial and ground, one who can fly

1Lt 'Kenny' Giroux enjoys a cigarette whilst standing alongside his P-38J-15 at Owi in September 1944. A future ten-kill ace, Giroux's scoreboard at that point denoted his probable victories with the P-47 in November 1943 and his two confirmed kills in May and July 1944 – the latter victory (an 'Oscar', claimed on 27 July). Note the eight bomb symbols, each of which represented a successful fighter-bomber mission (*via John Stanaway*)

a good formation and who has had lots of so-called 'rat-racing'. A pilot with that background who enters a squadron with an open mind, and who is intent on success will, with the help of the operations officer and flight leaders, have no trouble adapting himself to combat and will have every chance of returning to the States someday. A pilot who doesn't care for, or who has no great interest in pursuit flying, or who lacks the proper training, is starting with the cards stacked against him.

Capt William A Gardner
Operations Officer
8th FG

My first contacts with the enemy were in the latter part of 1943. The Japanese fighter formations were loose, and could be recognised in the distance as a swarm of flies. Many of the aeroplanes would flip momentarily onto their backs for a good look underneath, and others would be rolling.

In early 1944 there seemed to be a change in Japanese air tactics. Their bombers were doing most of their operating at night, and the fighter-bombers and fighters were trying our formations. On 16 January I was flying with a formation of 16 P-40Ns covering a landing at Saidor, New Guinea. Our four flights were stacked from 8000 to 14,000 ft.

Capt Bill Gardner (second from right) of the 35th FS explains how he became the first US pilot to land on the recently liberated airstrip at Tacloban, on Leyte Island, on 27 October 1944. Standing directly opposite him is Gen George C Kenney, Commander-in-Chief of the Fifth Air Force. Gardner was forced to make the impromptu landing at Tacloban after his Lightning was badly damaged by flak fired from a Japanese destroyer that his unit had attacked off Cebu (*via John Stanaway*)

William A Gardner

William A 'Bill' Gardner was born on 3 March 1920 in Gorham, New Hampshire. He graduated with a Bachelor of Science degree in mechanical engineering from the University of New Hampshire in 1941, immediately after which he joined the Army Reserves as a second lieutenant in the Coastal Artillery. Gardner transferred to the Army Air Corps in early 1942, and successfully completed pilot training on 10 November that same year. Undertaking his P-40 conversion training with the 10th FS/50th FG, the young pilot was posted to the Port Moresby-based 35th FS/8th FG on 1 September 1943.

Flying P-40N 42-105307 in the defence of New Guinea, he scored his first victory – a G4M 'Betty' bomber – near Finschhafen on 22 September. Gardner's next successes came on 16 January 1944, when he and 14 other P-40 pilots from the 35th FS engaged a mixed force of 40 Japanese fighters north of Saidor. Gardner downed three A6M 'Hamps' during the melee, which cost the enemy 19 aircraft in total – this was a record single mission score for a V Fighter Command squadron in World War 2.

The 35th FS re-equipped with P-38s in February 1944, and it was not until 16 June that Gardner got to score his all-important fifth kill (an A6M 'Zeke' whilst on a sweep of the Dutch East Indies) to give him ace status. He claimed a Ki-61 'Tony' on 27 July for his sixth victory and a K-21 'Sally' bomber on 17 August for his seventh. Gardner's final success took the form of another 'Zeke' (or possibly a 'Tojo') on 1 November, claimed over Negros Island during the Leyte campaign. With 172 combat missions behind him, Gardner was transferred from the 35th FS to 8th FG HQ as group operations officer shortly afterwards. He remained with the 8th until April 1945.

Post-war, Gardner left the USAAF and joined the Curtiss Propeller Division of Wright Aeronautical Corporation, where he served as its chief of flight testing until 1948. He then became involved in defence contracting with the fledgling US Air Force, overseeing numerous advanced weapon systems projects as the director of Sands National Laboratories in Albuquerque, New Mexico, until his retirement in 1984.

A young 1Lt Bill Gardner is seen with his P-40N-5 (possibly 42-105307) at Cape Gloucester sometime after claiming a trio of 'Hamp' victories on 16 January 1944. The future eight-kill ace had opened his account with a solitary 'Betty' bomber on 22 September 1943 – just three weeks after joining the 35th FS. A great advocate of the N-model Warhawk, Gardner was almost willing to declare that the fighter was the equal of the Merlin-engined Mustang at lower altitudes (*via John Stanaway*)

Approximately 40 Japanese fighters – 'Tonys', 'Hamps' and 'Zekes' – came in from about 16,000 ft in neat four-ship formations. The top and nearest flight called them in first, and turned into them. Our other flights started to gain altitude and turned into the enemy fighters as they came down through us. The Japanese made the mistake of losing their altitude advantage, and in the free-for-all that ensued, they lost 19 aeroplanes – we had just two holed. They kept their four-ship flight together, but their support seemed to go no further than that.

In combat against fighters, it is almost impossible to keep more than an element of two together, and frequently even this element may be broken down to climax a combat, but all aeroplanes are close enough together so the flights can be reformed after the fight. This can be in a Lufbery. It matters not who assumes the lead of the flights – just get together. A four-ship, with each aircraft in mutual support of the other, is the best defensive formation, but I believe that the minute this defence is turned into an offence (which should be as soon as contact is made), it is unwise to try and keep four-ships together.

Keep your head on a swivel and know what is going on around and behind you. If you see the enemy first, or when they are still a good distance away, you are never at a disadvantage.

Keep up plenty of speed. A Japanese fighter pilot can out-manoeuvre you at low speed, but at high speeds his controls get hard. A high-speed turn to the right will shake the best of them.

Don't fire too soon. You might scare off a good kill by shooting over his wing, and also waste shells that might come in handy later on.

Many lessons have been learned from the strafing and dive-bombing attacks we have carried out. Attacks on airfields and other heavily defended targets should be well planned. Fighters should come in abreast, giving as much firepower and coverage as possible. Japanese light and medium ack-ack gunners are good, and they get more accurate as they get more practice. On recent dive-bombing missions I have seen evidence of pre-cut fuses, where bursts of medium ack-ack follow or lead you in a dive all the way from 8000 ft down to 2000 ft.

I have one more item which has meant as much, or more, then all the others in coming back to fly another day. This is fuel conservation. Many of our missions in P-38s have been trips of 800 miles to the target, fight, and return with nothing but enemy territory or water to set down on if you miscalculated on your gas load. If you can't get to the target on your drop tanks then turn back, because you won't be able to make it back anyway if you use up gas in a scrap. When you do get caught up short, reduce RPM to as low as 1600, pull manifold pressure down to 24 or 25 inches of HG and bring your mixture control back beyond auto-lean to a point where you start to get a drop in RPM. Relax and head for home.

MAJ CYRIL F HOMER
80th FS/8th FG

All individual evasive action may vary greatly depending on the enemys' strength, their position to you and the type of aeroplane they are flying. It is sometimes hard to distinguish one type of enemy fighter from

Aces 1Lt Cy Homer (in P-38G-1 42-12705, coded 'V') and Maj 'Porky' Cragg (in P-38H-1 42-66835) escort 501st Bomb Squadron/345th Bomb Group B-25D-15 41-30594 as it heads for the Japanese stronghold of Rabaul on 2 November 1943. Cragg, who was CO of the 80th FS, claimed a 'Val' and a 'Zeke' probably destroyed during this mission. He was posted missing in action on 26 December 1943, having claimed 15 kills. Homer's score stood at five victories when this photograph was taken (*via John Stanaway*)

another. Consequently, in any case it is advisable to maintain an air speed of 300 mph or more until an altitude of at least 10,000 ft is attained, giving you room to dive out of trouble. Even though you may find yourself badly out-numbered, it is not necessary to leave at once. Attack is your best defence in the case of your being jumped. After a pass or two it will be easier to break away, for this will usually surprise the enemy.

Looking around, keeping your ship rolling and turning, is the best possible defence. As long as you see the enemy, his chances of nailing you are very slim. But in the case where you have not done this and find your tail is dirty, then is the time to get violent on the controls. A violent combined push-over and roll to the vertical position will likely throw him off until you can pick up diving speed. Twist, roll, reverse and jink until you have 400 mph or more – in case it's a 'Tony', 500 mph – then pull out level. Then you can easily outdistance him at this angle, or better yet, pull up into a shallow climb. Judge your lead carefully and reverse 180 degrees to him for a head-on pass, unless he is followed by some of his friends.

When caught just above the tree-tops or water at slow speed, you can only hope to throw his aim off by jerking and skidding, at the same time striving for altitude. Drop full flaps if necessary – anything to make him overshoot. Any of these cases can be eliminated as long as a pilot remains alert with a little altitude on his side. Join any friendly ships whenever possible, and keep your runs pointed at the enemy – not your tail.

Before taking on anything alone, give the situation a good looking over. Make sure that if you do attack, you are not also being followed. No matter how well you look around you, you will not see all the aeroplanes in the area. You sometimes feel as if they come out of nowhere. In the case of the enemy being below, judge his speed before coming down, then as you come down, roll around clearing yourself. Do not try to dive on him – instead, dive under and up from the rear, for this is his blind spot.

Cyril F Homer

Cyril Filcher 'Cy' Homer was born on 29 April 1919 in West New Jersey, New Jersey. Moving to the west coast as a youth, he attended the University of California before joining the Army Reserves. Homer then transferred to the Army Air Corps for flight training, and graduated as a pilot from Luke Field, Arizona, as part of Class 42-J on 30 October 1942. He transitioned onto the P-38 Lightning at Muroc Field (later renamed Edwards), in California, and was then sent to the 80th FS/8th FG at Mareeba, in Queensland, Australia, in February 1943, just as the squadron was transitioning from the P-39 to the P-38.

Homer's arrival raised some eyebrows amongst the battle-hardened veterans of the 80th FS, including flight commander Norbert Ruff, who remembered thinking that that the Army Air Force was scraping the bottom of the barrel by making a fighter pilot of this severe-looking man with a pronounced limp (just two years earlier an aviation cadet had had to be in perfect physical shape). Homer had raced motorcycles pre-war until he had been badly injured in a crash. All reservations vanished, however, when Ruff saw the most unbelievable manoeuvres executed by Homer's P-38, eventually coupled with some excellent shooting once the unit was sent back into combat.

The 80th FS returned to action from Port Moresby on 16 May 1943, and five days later Homer probably destroyed a Ki-43 'Oscar' north-east of Salamaua while flying 'his' P-38G-1 42-12705, christened *COTTON DUSTER*. He finally claimed his first confirmed kills – in P-38G-15 43-2386 – on 21 August when he destroyed two A6M 'Zekes' and a Ki-61 'Tony' over Wewak. Another 'Zeke' fell to his guns on 4 September, and Homer 'made ace' nine days later when he destroyed an 'Oscar'. Both kills were again claimed in 'his' P-38G-1 42-12705. Accompanying the group from Port Moresby to its new base at Finschhafen in December 1943, Homer continued to find the enemy to his liking over Wewak in the New Year, when he accounted for two 'Oscars' (on 18 and 23 January) and a 'Tony' (also on 23 January). Another 'Tony' was destroyed on 30 March, and Homer enjoyed his career high on 3 April when he downed two 'Oscars' and two 'Tonys' over Hollandia whilst flying a brand new P-38J-15. 'Uncle Cy', as the ace became known within the 80th FS, chalked up his 14th kill (a Ki-43) on 27 July and rounded out his aerial victories with yet another 'Oscar', over Leyte, on 10 November. By then he was CO of the 80th FS, having assumed command from 22-kill ace Capt Jay T Robbins on 4 October. Homer remained in this post until 9 May 1945, and he returned home later that same month.

Maj Cyril Homer left the service at the end of the war, and passed away on 10 August 1975, shortly after attending an 8th FG reunion.

Capt Cy Homer, by now CO of the 80th FS, poses for the base photographer at Morotai in late 1944 (*via John Stanaway*)

P-38G-1 42-12705 was the first Lightning assigned to Cy Homer upon his arrival in the Southwest Pacific, the fighter having been supplied new to the 80th FS in early 1943. Named *COTTON DUSTER*, *AVA* and *LILLY NELL*, it was routinely flown by Homer throughout 1943. Indeed, he claimed two kills and three probables with it between 21 May and 7 November. His remaining victories (three) for 1943 were scored in P-38G-15 43-2386 on 21 August. A colour profile of 42-12705 appears on page 66 (*via John Stanaway*)

An overhead pass usually gives you too much speed, and you can not turn as well with the nose pointed down as up.

Do not count on him for a set evasive action, for although he will usually half roll, he may on the other hand pull up or make a diving turn. Give yourself enough speed over him so that you can break away safely in case you miss, and no more. Too much speed will cut your firing time to zero. If he turns, break away and down as soon as you lose your lead, for he may reverse onto your tail as you go by. Climb back up as soon as you get out of range, then make a 180-degree head-on pass, but make sure you lead enough before attempting this reverse.

On a head-on pass, bore in and don't budge until collision appears inevitable. You should have done him in by this time, but if not, push under violently. The usual pilot will react by pulling up or to one side. Although pushing under is uncomfortable, I believe there is less chance of him doing likewise. Keep going straight till you know where he is. If he rolls coming in, you can expect to find him behind and underneath. A sharp pull-up and then hammerhead down on him is good, for he is, or should be, about stalled out. Never fire out of range. Firing out of range will give you away every time, whereas you might have closed in unobserved.

ALWAYS clear your tail before firing.
ALWAYS try to use the element of surprise.
ALWAYS close in, and then use short bursts.
ALWAYS take advantage of sun and cloud cover.
ALWAYS hit the enemy where they are thickest.
ALWAYS try to join with another friendly aeroplane.

When using the 16-ship squadron formation, each flight will be positioned to cover each other and each flight can also be seen and covered by the leader, the down-sun flights each being stacked about 500 ft or more above each other. The squadron must be led by a capable man who has the respect of his men. He should have seen combat, and be wise in it, for there is one way to prove yourself, and that is in actual combat. An example should be set for the men to follow.

As the flights are stacked, the foregoing flights are well covered, and the most vulnerable flight is the last and uppermost. Should he get bounced, he should take his men down beneath and behind the number three flight, which can in turn make a 180-degree turn into the aggressors. Element leaders should use a scissors manoeuvre, with the first element in a flight, as a four-man flight flying close cannot protect itself. If a fight develops, we advise four-ship flights to stay together, strung out well, so that the leader may clear number four man's tail by reversing.

It is sometimes nearly impossible to keep four-ships together, so that leaves elements. Two-ships working together can stand off large odds by using scissor and reverse manoeuvres, but their offensive value is low against numbers. I believe that a wingman should fly behind or to the side, spaced enough to allow the number one man to make a 180-degree turn to clear number two's tail.

Squadron leaders should attack aggressively and hit the enemy where they are the thickest, thus ensuring that all his men will get into the fight. Trying to pick off stragglers and high ones is not for the leader, for unless his flight leaders are overly eager, they will follow him and usually have nothing to shoot at. Before diving into anything, the leader should summarise their strength and position. If the enemy is strong in numbers, he may want to take his first eight ships down, leaving the last eight ships high and ready to come down. He should try to come out of the sun or use clouds – anything for surprise.

Flight leaders will space themselves well, with their elements the same, so they can pick off anything the leader may set up. Four-ships flying close together will usually get about the same results as one single ship.

Capt Homer is flanked by his crew chief, T/Sgt Mel 'Slim' Gardner (left) and assistant crew chief Sgt Ged Kicker at Morotai in November 1944. The men are standing in front of 'their' P-38J, whose serial remains unidentified. Although 16 victory decals adorn the fighter's fuselage, Homer was in fact only credited with 15 confirmed kills – he also claimed five probables and four damaged (*via John Stanaway*)

UNCLE CY's Angel taxies past a pair of P-47Ds from the 35th FG at Morotai in October 1944. Soon after being made CO of the 80th FS on 4 October, Homer had the rudders and outer horizontal tail surfaces of his faithful Lightning painted in green and white checks. Quite how he got official approval for this personal marking remains a mystery. A colour profile of this machine appears on page 66 (*via John Stanaway*)

CAPT ALLEN E HILL
36th FS/8th FG

I consider it a privilege to have an opportunity to pass on to those who may follow me the following information on combat flying. I hope that there might be one bit of experience that will help them.

My tactics have changed much from the first day I arrived in this theatre, when we were most generally outnumbered ten-to-one, to the present day when an equal number is hard to find. One must never hang on to old, obsolete tactics, but should alter them day by day to fit new types of enemy aircraft and situations.

My squadron, upon arriving into an area where combat is expected, is put in long string formation and weaves violently so that all aeroplanes are covered at all times.

In cases where we do the attacking, it is done by flights. Never do we split up in more than two-ship elements. If a man finds himself alone during a fight, he must join up with the nearest aeroplane, no matter who it is. A two-ship element is five times as powerful as two single aeroplanes flying alone, and ten times safer.

Our tactics in fighting are simple – keep up your airspeed, hit and run, so you can hit again. Never dogfight with Japanese aircraft. Remember, his one aim is to make you lose airspeed so he can then have the advantage. It is permissible to follow one in a tight turn as long as you can hold your lead, but as he slips through your sights, break off your attack immediately.

Not always are you the attacking aircraft, however. In cases where he is doing the bouncing, always try to make it at least a head-on pass. A head-on pass is without a doubt the acme of fighter pilot thrills, but remember there are some Japanese pilots who will not break away, so don't hold your fire too long. You have far greater range and firepower and can stay right in there and pitch until the last second. In most cases, if he is going to break, he will do it out of your range, giving you a snapshot as he breaks.

In cases where you are really latched, it doesn't matter much what you do, but *do something, and do it violently.* The old Japanese trick of 'split-S'ing' is good, using a violent skid going down. As you pick up airspeed, start a fast climb away, always maintaining over 200 mph. Now you are ready for the attacking.

In cases where a flight is attacked, a scissoring movement of the elements is a good tactic. It makes the attacker commit himself to one or the other, leaving the other element free to turn into him.

Remember, good formation is good life insurance. Very seldom is a formation that looks good attacked but lo' the man who trails.

Altitude is your greatest asset. It can be turned into airspeed and surprise at your choosing. Not only that, but you are flying an aeroplane that was meant to do its flying upstairs.

Allen E Hill

Allen E Hill was born on 7 April 1918 in Sterling, Illinois. He joined the Army Reserves in early 1942 and immediately applied for flight training with the Army Air Corps. Presented with his wings on 4 January 1943 at Luke Field, Arizona, Hill completed his fighter transition in the United States and was then posted as an attrition replacement to the 80th FS/8th FG at Port Moresby on 3 September. Just ten days later he scored his first aerial victory, downing an A6M 'Zeke' over Wewak in P-38G-15 43-2382.

Belying his limited combat experience, Hill enjoyed further successes in the coming months over Rabaul, destroying four more 'Zekes' to 'make ace' in a series of engagements on 29 October and 2 (two destroyed and a third probably destroyed) and 7 November. His run of victories then dried up, and he scored just a solitary kill during the next eight months – a Ki-61 'Tony' over Wewak on 18 January 1944. Things picked up in July, when he downed a Ki-43 'Oscar' on the 27th and a D3A 'Val' dive-bomber on the 29th.

Hill was promoted to captain in September and transferred to the 36th FS as commanding officer on 15 November 1944. He scored his ninth, and last, victory when he destroyed an 'Oscar' over Mindoro, in the Philippines, on 20 December. Promoted to major in March 1945, Allen Hill was declared tour-expired three months later and sent home. He left the Army Air Force soon after returning to the USA.

1Lt Allen Hill and P-38J-10 42-67898 at Finschhafen in late January 1944. Note the chalked outline of the *Hill's Angels* artwork which would soon adorn the nose of this early-build J-model. Hill almost certainly claimed his sixth kill (a Ki-61) in this aircraft on 18 January. A colour profile of 42-67898 appears on page 66 (*via William Hess*)

A nude named *Wilful Winnie* also graced the starboard side of Hill's P-38J-10, as did the salivating Snow White dwarf 'Dopey'. Hill is joined in this photograph by a cigar-chewing Capt Dwinell (first name unknown) (*via John Stanaway*)

One factor which counts more to the success of the mission than anything else is how well each pilot is briefed on the mission on which he is about to go. A pilot that doesn't know what is going on might as well be back in camp.

I think I need not go into shooting, as everyone has heard a dozen or more times to get into range. Anyone can shoot an aeroplane down, but not everyone can hit them at 600 yards. Most generally, your first shot is your last shot at Japanese aircraft.

I could also go into detail on strafing. Strafing will cost us more pilots than aerial combat, but with a little common sense it need not be you. Never get so intent on your target that you forget you are flying an aeroplane. You will be called upon to strafe many enemy installations where anti-aircraft guns are present, so naturally we can't peel up to become sitting ducks, but instead we peel away flat and on the treetops. Our attacks are most generally coordinated with someone strafing the gun emplacements and someone else the target – each with the same importance.

You will have fun flying combat, and when it ceases to be fun or hold a thrill for you, look up your flight surgeon, because you are no longer a combat pilot.

35th FIGHTER GROUP

COL EDWIN A DOSS
COMMANDING OFFICER
35th FG

On offensive sweeps the diamond type of squadron formation is flown. A fight always starts in one of two ways – either the squadron goes down to attack, or the squadron is itself attacked, usually from above. The flights should be dispersed to give maximum protection to everyone involved. In the event that there are only a few enemy aeroplanes, the squadron leader can despatch one or two flights to deal with the enemy, the remaining flights taking a position off to one side so that maximum coverage of the fight may be maintained. The flights should be into the sun if possible. In case a large number of enemy aeroplanes are sighted, a squadron attack should be delivered, provided we have the initial advantage. NEVER start a fight at a disadvantage.

After contact is made, a squadron formation is impossible to maintain, whereupon the fighting breaks down into flights, and even further to elements and individual combat. A man fighting alone is at a definite disadvantage and is uncalled for. Every effort should be made to maintain a flight formation at all times.

Flights are many times unavoidably split up, in which case the elements should remain intact, and should attempt to rejoin into a flight formation as soon as possible. The enemy thinks twice before attacking a well formed flight, whereas an individual is always in trouble avoiding the enemy, who invariably 'gang up' on the individual fighter. In individual flight combat, full advantage of the aeroplane must be taken at all times, and combat where the enemy is superior must be avoided.

35th FG CO Lt Col Edwin Doss (centre) is presented with coffee and sandwiches by 41st FS CO Maj Douglas Parsons after the completion of a successful sortie in 1944. The date of this photograph remains unrecorded, although a hand-written note by Doss on the reverse of the print stated that the group had claimed 32 victories during the course of the day, hence the smiles on the pilots' faces (*via Jim Doss*)

This may seem obvious, but to elucidate, we know that the enemy fighters are much superior in turning, and possess a remarkable ability to hang on their props. Our fighters are much superior in high climbs and shallow dives. Below 15,000 ft, the rate of climb at high angle favours the enemy. But our fighters are capable of climbing from 2300 to 3300 ft/min at 200 mph. For the enemy to maintain the above mentioned rate of climb, his indicated speed must of necessity be in the neighbourhood of 150 mph. Hence we possess a 50-mph speed advantage. In using the speed advantage, and an attack is made, the flight pulls away in a high-speed climb, then turns about for another attack.

It is a great temptation to follow an enemy fighter in a climb, and it is possible to do so for a short distance. Never get below 200 mph in a

Edwin A Doss

Edwin Allen Doss was born in Rector, Arkansas, on 14 September 1914. He graduated from Portageville High School in Missouri in 1932 and Lead Belt Junior College, Desloge, again in Missouri, in 1936. Doss entered Army Air Corps aviation cadet pilot training in April 1940, graduating from Kelly Field, Texas, on 20 December 1940 with the rank of second lieutenant. His first military assignment was to the P-35-equipped 41st Pursuit Squadron of the 31st Pursuit Group, based at Selfridge Field, Michigan. In April 1941 Doss was promoted to squadron operations officer, and in January 1942 he accompanied his squadron on its deployment to the SWPA (South West Pacific Area). Here, the group was issued with Airacobras at Port Moresby, and thrown into the defence of the New Guinean capital. By now a captain, Doss was designated squadron commander of the 41st in June 1942, and he led the unit during the critical air combat phase of the campaign. His rise through the ranks continued in 1943, when he was promoted to major in March 1943.

In August 1943 Doss assumed command of the 35th FG, and was promoted to lieutenant colonel the following November. It was at around this time that his group re-equipped with P-47 Thunderbolts, which replaced P-38s, P-39s and P-400s. In the succeeding months, he led the 35th through the most intensive and bitterly fought campaigns of the Pacific theatre of operations, from Lae, New Guinea, to Okinawa. In March 1945, Doss was promoted to full colonel, and during this month his group swapped its P-47Ds for P-51D Mustangs.

Returning to the United States in late July 1945, Doss was assigned to Selfridge Field as Chief of Staff of the 62nd FW. In August 1947 he was designated to command the F-51 Mustang-equipped 27th FG upon its formation at Kearney, Nebraska, before returning to Selfridge in January 1949 to serve as the Deputy for Reserve Forces, Headquarters Tenth Air Force. The following July Doss became the Senior Air Force Advisor to the 66th FW of the Illinois Air National Guard, and from June 1951 to January 1953 served as an Air Force member of the Weapons Systems Evaluation Group, Office of the Secretary of Defense.

climbing combat, and in level flight 250 mph is a good speed which affords a maximum of protection and manoeuvrability. In combat it is impossible to maintain complete coverage of the area, and usually when a flight, or individual, gets below 200 mph, he is setting himself up for the enemy. Remember that steep angle, low speed climbs are nothing short of sheer suicide. Above 2000 ft the advantage in climb favours our fighters.

The enemy always attempts to get into circle combat, and this should be avoided. 'Fancy' manoeuvres, though pretty to watch, are invitations to disaster. The enemy does not like to swap head-on passes because of our superior firepower. Care should be exercised to initiate the breakaway not because of the suicidal intentions of the enemy pilot, but should he be dead, mid-air collisions are likely to result. The breakaway should be

After completing a jet transition course at Craig Air Force Base, Col Doss was designated as CO of the 49th Fighter Bomber Wing at Kunsan, Korea, in March 1953. Then equipped with F-84G Thunderjets, the group had been waging war in Korea since 1950, and Doss once again assumed the role of a combat commander as he led his wing through the remainder of the campaign. Having flown over 230 missions in World War 2, by war's end he had increased his tally to 280, totalling 573 hours. Following the cease-fire agreement, he was assigned to command the B-26 Invader-equipped 3rd Bomber Wing at Kunsan, Korea. Following his return to the US in April 1954, Doss held successive assignments as Senior Air Force Advisor to the Pennsylvania Air National Guard, Vice Commander of the 85th Air Division (Air Defense) at Andrews Air Force Base and Deputy Commander of the Washington Air Defense Sector at Fort Lee, Virginia. In April 1960 Col Doss was designated as commander of the Bangor Air Defense Sector, and he served concurrently as CO of the Bangor Continental and Bangor North American Air Defense Sectors.

In July 1963 Col Doss was assigned to Headquarters USAFE. Here, he served as Deputy Inspector General and Inspector General until 1 July 1964, when he was designated to head the command liaison agency to the government of France, in Paris. He finally retired from the USAF in 1968. Edwin Doss died in 1995, aged 81.

Lt Col Doss (left) poses with his deputy group commander, Lt Col F S Wagner, outside the 35th FG's HQ building at Gusap in February 1944. Wagner led the group from 12 February through to 4 May 1944 while Ed Doss enjoyed well-earned leave in the USA (*via Jim Doss*)

affected at high speeds, since the enemy has the ability to whip onto your tail if another attack is attempted before a safe distance out has been reached.

When the flight is attacking the enemy, should he start a severe turn, the lead element will usually break away, thus giving the second element an opportunity to get in a shot, after which it too breaks away, then joins the lead element again. The same is true for wingmen. There are numerous occasions where the wingman can get in the only effective shot. It is a bad policy to press the attack for any length of time, because while being absorbed in making the attack, other enemy fighters may have time to make an attack upon you while you are not looking.

It is not considered good policy to sacrifice a great deal of altitude in order to press home an attack, particularly when there are many enemy fighters in the area. There are usually enough enemy fighters on the same flight level to afford plenty of combat. Maintaining altitude is like money in the bank – when you don't have any, you usually wish you did have some. This does not always hold true, but it should be borne in mind at all times.

When the squadron makes an attack, it is desirable if possible to have one flight hold back for a while to act as top protection in case hitherto unseen enemy fighters attempt to join in the fight.

When pulling rated power, except in extreme emergencies, the flight leader should allow four inches leeway for the rest of the flight. Experience has shown that to be sufficient for well schooled pilots.

When the squadron is attacked from above, the only alternative usually open to the top flight is to dive away. The squadron should never have so little warning that one of the lower flights cannot make a turn into the attackers. When the formation is of the typical diamond, the flight that is furthest away and down has the most time to avoid attack by turning and forcing the enemy into a head-on pass. The intermediate ones may have time to turn sufficiently to fire a few bursts, which sometimes scares them off. That ruse does not always work, however, but the flight can always dive away if the disadvantage is too great. Owing to the high rate of roll and high push-over rate of the P-47, the best breakaway if attacked from 'six o'clock' at fairly close range is to shove the stick into the right hand corner. It is impossible for the enemy, despite his great manoeuvrability, to apply sufficient lead to get a good shot. When a top flight dives away, it should do so under the other flights of the formation in order for the other flights to ward off the attack.

After the combat has gone on for 15 minutes, the squadron leader will give the radio signal for the squadron to clear the area and reform. The flight leaders should obey immediately so as to reduce the forming time to a minimum. This saves gallons of gasoline, which is very important if operating at the extreme range of the aeroplane. The maximum daily operating range of the P-47D-28 is 750 miles.

DIVE-BOMBING TACTICS OF THE P-51 IN THE SWPA

During the past few months this group has done considerable work in close support of the ground forces. These missions include dive-bombing, skip-bombing and strafing. The tactics employed vary with the type of target and the anti-aircraft fire expected.

The P-51 type aircraft is relatively new to this theatre. However, from our limited experience with this type of aeroplane, we find it to be the ideal weapon for this type of work, as well as being a superior aircraft for escort missions and fighter sweeps. The following discussion will be confined to tactics used with the P-51.

Bomb loads and fusing depends entirely upon the type of target to be attacked. Our best results have been obtained using two 500- or 600-lb fragmentation clusters. For dive-bombing runways and landing strips, we use a 110-second delay fuse. On all other dive-bombing missions an instantaneous fuse is used. For skip-bombing missions, a three- to five-second delay fuse is necessary. The types of targets we have attacked by dive-bombing and strafing include airfields, bivouac areas, troop concentrations, ammunition and supply dumps, large bridges and many similar targets. Skip-bombing attacks have been limited to small bridges, warehouses and important enemy installations.

Our approach for dive-bombing is made at 6000 ft, using evasive action going in. A steep dive is used with power off. The bombs are released at about 2000 ft. On targets where little anti-aircraft fire is expected, we have found that ten degrees of flap gives a slower diving speed and increases the bombing accuracy. Our breakaway is normal, using evasive action on the way out. On close support missions, panels are used to mark the location of our troops and smoke is used to mark the target. All attacks are made parallel to our own frontlines.

We have had great success in destroying many ground targets by coordinated attacks, with half of the flight dive-bombing and the other half skip-bombing at low level. By using these tactics, we have destroyed practically every target without a loss of pilot or aeroplane.

MAJ JOHN R YOUNG
OPERATIONS OFFICER
35th FG

My experience has been varied in the 28 months I have been in this theatre – in fact so varied that my knowledge is only general with regards to the usual types of combat tactics.

Since my only successful kills were on long range fighter sweeps coordinated with Liberator strikes, I will mention only the tactics as used on this particular type of work. In some cases, sound policy was slightly side-tracked, but only for the purpose of increasing range, which goes hand in hand with an added safety factor in getting home safely.

The missions I use as an example were P-47 fighter sweeps designed to clear the target area of Japanese fighters at the moment Liberators were coming in to do their job. This particular target was 835 statute miles from our nearest base. In order to reach the target and lend any assistance to the bombers, it was necessary to equip the P-47s with three external tanks. The wing tanks were dropped as emptied, while the 75-gallon belly tanks were kept during the entire combat with the enemy. It was obvious that even with the added gasoline supply, it was necessary for each pilot to use every trick we had developed in conserving fuel to reach the target with the required fuel to return to base.

35th FG Operations Officer Maj 'Johnny' Young had served as CO of the group's 40th FS from 5 May through to 8 November 1944, before joining the HQ staff. Although the P-47 that he is sat in bears five victory decals, Young was not officially listed as an ace, so these kills may signify probables or ground strafing successes. As previously noted, 'Johnny' Young was killed in a freak accident at Clark Field, in the Philippines, in May 1945. A 35th FG P-51 lost a napalm tank on take-off, and the store skidded across the runway and hit Maj Young's jeep. Despite the pilot's best efforts to evade the tank, he was badly burned when the napalm exploded upon impact with the jeep. Young succumbed to his injuries a week later

We used much thought and ran many tests developing our procedure for reaching the target, and it will no doubt be criticised by many. The primary aim was to produce the maximum striking power over the target area, and remain there as long as possible. Since the mission required eight-and-one-half hours of flying time, it was necessary to operate the aeroplane at its most economical power setting, for fuel meant striking power. But at the same time we could not disregard the fact that a fresh, alert pilot was also needed to produce this striking power.

It was proven by test that our best range could be obtained by taking off and proceeding to the target very close to the deck. This required more flying time than it would have at altitude to complete the mission, and also had the disadvantage of tiring the pilot because of the intense heat experienced in the cockpit of a P-47 while flying low in this theatre. In the end, we compromised and flew out at 7000 ft. This altitude had the added advantage of being below the oxygen level.

The formation, going out, was flown very wide, thus allowing each pilot to fly his aeroplane in comfort. This also allowed him to get the most economical power settings for his particular aeroplane, and it took only an occasional change in prop setting to keep in place. We began climbing at a point that enabled us to reach 20,000 ft 15 minutes from the target area. This was considered ample, for the Japanese doesn't like to meet us at altitude, and in this case even provided enough height to jump them with plenty of speed.

After levelling out at 20, 000 ft, we immediately went into combat formation, stressing two-ship elements with wingmen flying just far enough out to give cover to his leader and still enable him to look around. At this point the success of the mission depended on one thing – spotting the enemy first. This was a must, and we did. Then we jumped him fast and hit him hard, each pilot closing for a sure kill, thus avoiding waste of fire and time by scaring him off while out of range. Elements immediately pulled up, regaining some of the altitude lost in the jump, reformed and pressed a second attack just as ferocious as the first.

This fast, hard-hitting policy was essential as we had fuel for only ten minutes of combat – even less if forced to scrap our way out. From the pilot standpoint also, it was much more comfortable to be the aggressor while carrying a belly tank in combat.

After our second vicious attack, the enemy's plan of attack was broken. Only a few individual passes were made on single enemy aircraft in the area as we proceeded on our long trip home. Because of our hard-hitting policy, we were able to keep the enemy entirely on the defensive, with the result that our pilots bagged a number of aircraft and the bombers completed their own mission with less resistance.

In concluding, I would like to bring out the fact that the superiority of the P-47 over the enemy in speed and firepower, plus the superiority of our pilots in seeing and pressing the attack, enabled us to run a mission of this length with such a limited amount of fuel allowed for actual combat. We must all use this to its fullest advantage. See the enemy first and hit him fast and hard. By doing this, we can press the attack closer and closer to the heart of the enemy in his homeland.

Aggressiveness is the fighter pilot's key to success, so be aggressive at all times.

CAPT LEROY V GROSSHUESCH
39th FS/35th FG

I'd like to start my letter concerning my personal viewpoint on combat tactics by stating just what capabilities and knowledge I think a good combat fighter pilot should have. A valuable pilot to a squadron should be able to see, not just scan the sky, but see everything. See the enemy before he sees you and it's a cinch. With our aeroplanes possessing superior speed and climbing ability, it also sets up a perfect defence.

A good pilot must be able to fly a good tactical formation. When the leader makes a violent manoeuvre to get an opponent, or to get away from him, it's better to look around and see your wingman protecting you than to see him off in the distance at the mercy of six or seven Zeros or 'Franks'.

A pilot has to know his aeroplane. He must know what it can do against the enemy. He must also know how to operate it efficiently. We have stretched our range in the P-47D-16, P-47D-21 and P-47D-23 to a 750-mile radius of action. Take 1500 miles, add to that a good 15-minute fight, and you have to watch your step to stretch that gasoline supply.

The right attitude is essential to a fighter pilot. When attacking an enemy aircraft I always try to position myself above and behind. However, any approach will work except a sharp climb into the enemy, which would

Capt Leroy Grossheusch lends scale to the sheer bulk of his P-47D-23 (42-278??) at Mangaldan, on Luzon, in February 1945. The eight-kill ace adorned all of his fighters with the number 33, and he almost certainly claimed six of his eight victories in this very machine between 30 January and 25 February 1945 (*via Leroy Grossheusch*)

The 39th FS/35th FG is seen up in squadron strength over New Guinea in mid 1944, each four-ship formation being lead by a diagonally-striped P-47D flown by a flight leader (*via John Stanaway*)

cut down your speed. At a low speed, with our comparatively poor manoeuvrability, we are in the enemy's element. A good Japanese pilot can make you look silly if you give him the chance. I've seen one 'split-S' and end up on his attacker's tail. This happened to a pilot in our squadron whose wingman was asleep. While he was shooting at the enemy leader, the

Leroy V Grosshuesch

Leroy Victor Grosshuesch was born on 6 May 1920 in Menno, South Dakota. A graduate of Yankton High School in Yankton, South Dakota, he attended the University of Maryland and Jackson State Teachers' College prior to joining the Army Reserves on 9 January 1942 at Fort Des Moines, Iowa. Serving in the enlisted ranks of the Quartermaster Corps until 4 October, Grosshuesch then commenced pilot training at Craig Field in Selma, Alabama. Graduating on 28 July 1943 and commissioned as a second lieutenant, he was posted to the 439th FS at Dale Mabry Field in Tallahassee, Florida, where he undertook his conversion onto the P-47. Grosshuesch was duly sent to the Southwest Pacific Area to serve with the 39th FS/35th FG, arriving in Port Moresby in early November 1943.

Few enemy aircraft were encountered during his first year in-theatre, and it was not until 21 November 1944 (by which time he was acting CO of the 39th FS) that he claimed his first kill when he downed a Ki-46 'Dinah' over the Negros Island chain. Two more kills followed on 30 January 1945 during a long-range fighter sweep of Formosa from the group's new base on Luzon, in the Philippines. Grosshuesch destroyed two 'biplane trainers' of unidentified type west of Taicha airfield, and when the 35th FG returned to Formosa on 10 February, he claimed a further two 'biplane' kills, as well as a lone Ki-46, to take his overall tally to six victories. Fifteen days later he achieved his seventh, and final, kill in a Thunderbolt when he destroyed a lone 'Dinah' west of Formosa. The Ki-46 crashed after

Capt Grossheusch and his crew chief (unnamed) signal their delight at the former's three-victory haul over Formosa on 10 February 1945. These kills boosted his tally to six, thus giving him ace status. A colour profile of this aircraft appears on page 67 (*via Leroy Grossheusch*)

latter's wingman did a lopsided loop and filled our own wingman full of holes. I underline this fact – *keep your speed up and never chop your throttle*. One good burst will finish him anyway.

Never, never try to manoeuvre with the enemy. If he chandelles or does a 'split-S' he makes a perfect snapshot for your wingman, providing he is

sunset, thus qualifying Grosshuesch as the first (and only?) pilot to score a night victory in a P-47.

Missions to Formosa had been considered out of the question for the 'short-legged' P-47 until the 35th FG had hosted Charles Lindbergh for two weeks in July 1944. He taught the pilots the art of cruise control in the Thunderbolt, as he had previously done for P-38 crews in-theatre. In a matter of days Lindbergh had helped the group extend its radius of our action from 350 to 500 miles. Grosshuesch continued to work on this procedure, finally increasing the radius of action for his squadron to a staggering 800 miles. This proved to be a pivotal turning point in the war for the P-47s in the Southwest Pacific, allowing them to reach the more active areas of combat.

The group swapped its much-loved P-47s for P-51Ds in March 1945, and in its remaining months in combat the 35th FG moved bases on several occasions in an effort to stay in touch with the enemy. The group finally ended up on Okinawa in late June 1945, and on 30 July Capt Grosshuesch was credited with single-handedly sinking a Japanese destroyer off Goto Retto, near Kyushu. Thirteen days later he claimed his last kill when he destroyed a Ki-84 'Frank' west of Bofu airfield, on the Japanese mainland. By war's end he had flown 150 combat missions, 624 combat hours and a total of 1021 flying hours in P-47s and P-51s.

Having spent time in Japan post-war, Grosshuesch returned to the United States in August 1946 and was tendered a regular appointment in the US Army with the rank of captain – he was reassigned to the 61st FS/56th FG at Selfridge Field, Michigan, flying P-51s. In April 1947 Grosshuesch was transferred to the 335th FS/4th FG at Andrews Field, Washington, DC, where he flew the P-80 whilst serving as the squadron's executive officer. Ground tours in Turkey and Washington, DC followed, until he returned to the cockpit in July 1954 when he reported for duty as CO of the 452nd Day Fighter Squadron at Foster AFB, in Texas. Returning to the Pacific in June 1955, Col Grosshuesch served as CO of the 36th Fighter Bomber Squadron/51st Fighter Bomber Group at Itazuke air base, Japan, until June 1958, flying the F-86F and F-100.

Following more ground tours in the United States, he transferred to the Air Force Section, US Mission Vietnam, in Saigon and Nha Trang in July 1964, where Grosshuesch served as Commander, Special Air Operations Group. His final years in the USAF were spent in staff positions with the Pacific Air Forces, Grosshuesch finally retiring in May 1973. He was then employed by the Weyer-haeuser Paper Company of Honolulu, Hawaii, as sales manager, where he remained until his final retirement in July 1992. Col Leroy Grosshuesch and his wife reside in Kaneohe, Hawaii.

properly spaced. My advice is if you don't get him on your first pass, pull off to the side and climb at 200 mph. After you have your altitude come back and do it again. The wingman and element leaders usually get good chances at the enemy fighter when he breaks, and are then able to fall right back into formation. I'd never refuse a head-on pass – our superior firepower in the P-47 will take care of that.

I'd like to say here that I believe that 50 per cent of Japanese pilots today are stupid novices. During a recent mission, four 'Franks' flew a beautiful formation while we shot them down one by one. The other five broke up, but used no evasive action. They too were shot down. The other fifty 50 per cent are usually exceptional pilots, and will give you trouble if you don't use your head. I observed one that accidentally meet a flight head-on. The flight was cruising. The Jap started turning as he passed alongside and was able to get enough of a burst at the last man to hole him.

As to individual defence, the best defence is to stay on the offensive. If one does get on your tail and you are in a desperate situation, skid and slip like mad. Their gunnery is not so hot in my estimation. This might be some consolation. However, the best method of getting away in the P-47 is to climb at 200 mph at maximum power. You will pull away rapidly, and soon have enough altitude advantage or distance to come back at him. Never allow yourself to be alone for they pick on stragglers.

Our squadron usually consists of four flights of four P-47s each – a flight on each side of the lead flight, approximately 1000 yards away, and the last flight behind, but in such a position that it can always be seen by the leader. These flights stack up from 1000 to 2000 ft. The squadron leader calls the attack and usually makes the first pass. However, it has paid us good dividends to send the flight that sees the enemy first down to save time. I believe that surprise is just another advantage to us. Many times I've followed my wingman or element leader into the attack because I couldn't see his bandit.

If the enemy force is near our size, or smaller, we usually send down numbers one and two flights. Number three flight comes down a short while later to pick off the stragglers and those getting away at the sides of the battle. Number four flight acts as top cover, but gets into the fight at the end if the sky is clear above. This flight can also get any one out of difficulty that needs it. We attempt to keep the flights together. The enemy, however, usually splits up, making it advisable to split into elements to get them all, but we never get below the two-man element. The wingman's job is to protect the leader. He falls back a little and to one side. This gives him the opportunity to pick out an enemy aircraft besides the leader's victim, or to get the enemy when he turns to avoid the leader's bullets.

For defence, the flights are spaced in such a manner that they can turn into another flight. This will break up the enemy's attack because you can turn into him, while the flight that is attacked can dive under you. Number four flight is in a position to protect any flight. If he is jumped, he can dive through the formation, which gives him speed, and at the same time one of the other flights can turn head-on into the enemy, which usually discourages them.

I'd like to relate a little incident here. For nearly an hour, eight P-47s protected a group of bombers from approximately 30 Japanese 'Tonys' and 'Zekes'. The enemy fighters continually made passes with two or three ships from all sides. Our defence was to turn into them. They would immediately break away, and we could continue over the bombers, but after a while their uneagerness and lack of coordination got the better of them and they left.

Our favourite defence, if the enemy is seen in time, is to climb the whole squadron out of danger, then to come back and attack the Japanese fighters from above.

In conclusion, I would like to point out a few things that should be known about the Japanese. The speed of their fighters is below that of ours, so superior speed is our greatest advantage. They have a good rate of climb, but we can out-climb them if they maintain our speed. The advantages here are obvious. The enemy can out-manoeuvre us easily, so avoid manoeuvring. His firepower is below ours, so don't hesitate to make a head-on pass. His protection is poor, thus a good burst in the wing roots will usually cause an explosion, The Jap has a tendency to panic. He doesn't usually use his head, and he's uneager and has poor coordination.

If the American pilot uses his head, uses his aeroplane properly and sees the enemy first, he has him licked before the fight begins.

CAPT WILLIAM H STRAND
40th FS/35TH FG

The principle feature of the Japanese fighter pilot in this theatre is the excellent manoeuvrability of his aircraft and his poor teamwork in combat. The following points discussed herein are tactics used by the 35th FG in combat, operating with P-47s,

With the increasing tempo of the Fifth Air Force offensive, longer range became imperative, and in the past few months the range of the P-47 has been lengthened from 350 miles to 800 miles, giving new life to heavy bombardment. Through experimentation, it has been found that the P-47D-28 with three tanks is perfectly capable of escort or a fighter sweep of 800 miles, but in this the fighter tactics as a group must be changed to some extent.

We have learned to fight while retaining our auxiliary tanks, and to use lower power settings in interception. Mass attacks on interceptors makes this possible, which of course leads back to one thing – the saving of gas. It must be remembered that mass teamwork is the keystone of long-range escort on fighter missions.

On bomber escort missions, when jumped from above we have found it best to turn into the enemy and spread out into two-ship elements and then reform immediately after first contact. Do not break away from the bombers because you have then lost your protection strength.

It is best to maintain 200 mph IAS (Indicated Air Speed) or above, so as to be able to move about the bombers quickly. Long-range bomber escort is ticklish work, and gas conservation must be considered at all times. You can't be too aggressive toward the enemy before the bombers reach the target because they will end up over the target without cover.

If jumped on during a fighter sweep, we hold squadron formation until after first contact, then break up into elements. This way we have a better chance of doing more damage and remaining in the scrap over the target

William H Strand

William H 'Wild Bill' Strand was born in Pasadena, California, on 22 August 1921. He attended Pasadena Junior College prior to joining the Army Reserves on 10 March 1942. Commissioned a pilot on 12 April 1943 at Luke Field, in Arizona, he was sent to the 35th FG's 40th FS in Port Moresby as an attrition replacement in August of that same year. Flying the P-39N-5, Strand achieved his first kill near Nadzab on 7 November when he downed a Ki-43, and claimed a second as probably destroyed.

His unit re-equipped with P-47Ds soon after his encounter with the 'Oscars', and on 4 March Strand was credited with damaging another Ki-43 over Wewak. In the autumn of 1944 the 35th FG commenced long-range missions against enemy airfields and installations in the Philippines, the Halmahera and Borneo from its base on Morotai. Flown as part of the preparation for the US invasion of the Philippines, these sorties saw the group enjoy great success while escorting B-24s on raids against the oil refineries at Balikpapan, in Borneo. Indeed, 'Wild Bill' Strand 'made ace' during the course of two such missions in October, downing three 'Oscars' over Manggar on the 10th and two more over Balikpapan four days later. His final kill came on 21 November when he destroyed a B6N 'Jill' naval attack bomber over Bacolod, in the Negros Island chain.

Remaining in the Army Air Force post-war, Bill Strand saw further combat flying F-51s in Korea. Shot down by flak on 10 April 1951, he successfully evaded capture and returned to Allied lines. Having completed his tour of duty, Strand was subsequently assigned to the USAF's Test Pilot Performance School, before returning to frontline flying with the F-80 Shooting Star-equipped 72nd FS/56th FG at Selfridge Air Base, in Michigan, in late 1951. He then served with a guided missile squadron, prior to retiring in 1960.

Moving back to California, Strand became an earthwork contractor before taking full retirement in the 1980s. He passed away in 2002.

Ranking ace of the 35th FG's 40th FS, 'Wild Bill' Strand scored a solitary kill in the P-39N-5 and six victories in the P-47D. He is seen here climbing onto the wing of a well-weathered Thunderbolt at Gusap in early 1944

longer with the limitations which we have. We form up and leave the target with the squadron leader at his request. This also holds true when we jump the enemy.

An airspeed above 200 mph IAS on fighter sweeps is a must, because in so doing you are maintaining a speed in the higher range of Jap fighters.

Let me express again that effective teamwork has been the reason for such success as this group has enjoyed whilst conducting long range fighter operations.

MAJ DOUGLAS V N PARSONS
DEPUTY COMMANDER
35th FG

Fighter tactics in general have basic principles which hold true no matter what the theatre. These principles stem from the nine Principles of War, but in the air over here, I would stress the Offensive, Economy of Force, Surprise and Simplicity angles.

Having served 28 months in this area, I have seen the V Fighter Command tactics change through progressive stages. In the early days at Port Moresby we were still on the defensive, seeking to protect our lone remaining New Guinea air base. We had just started to spread out as we closed on Buna, and worked out of Wau towards Salamaua and Lae. Then, we were equipped with P-39Ds and P-40s – hopelessly outclassed by the Japanese 'Zekes', 'Oscars' and 'Hamps', except in diving, pilot protection and firepower. Accordingly, as did Gen Chennault, we adopted tactics of diving into, or breaking down from any attack, carrying through with speed, climbing, turning and attacking again. This meant many head-on passes, but we had the enemy on that score with our cannon. Dogfighting or turning of course were out. Scrambles over Moresby meant maximum altitude, and with sufficient time we managed to get up to 26,000 ft. By keeping speed up, and by boldness and good feinting, our squadron managed to shoot down some bombers.

Of course, we were better off below 10,000 ft, but then we often had no choice. The premium was on good formation and teamwork, alertness and aggressiveness. Can you do better today? The two-ship element was never split – a form of life insurance that any fighter pilot who lived learned to appreciate. It called for real discipline. We eventually got P-39Ns, with more speed and climb, and we could advance our tactics a notch. It was then, in August 1943, that our men destroyed 12 out of 12 'Helens' over Tsili Tsili in less than one-and-one-half minutes. We no longer needed to break down, because by keeping our airspeed up, we could now out-climb our honourable opponent. But we were still cagey and cautious. To my knowledge, our tactics cost us only one pilot, and he was off by himself. Unfortunately, I had yet to see combat.

Knowledge gives you more of a safety factor than is often realised, particularly when actual experience is lacking, or yet to be gained. A pilot should constantly be teaching himself. Lying around at night, or while on the alert, he does well to pour through every bit of intelligence material that comes his way.

He should read every account of air fights between Japanese and Allied aeroplanes, or of escort tactics, analysing the techniques used by both sides – and then practice them in the air whenever possible. He should read technical data on the enemy aeroplanes, and learn their defensive arcs of fire as well as our effective fields of fire. He should learn terrain, to help when the compass goes out, or weather makes the return to base a little tougher. He should learn escape routes, etc. He should know the Intelligence and Operations file as well as their officers do. He should dream of situations in a theoretical fight, and figure his plan of attack or evasion. He should know his aeroplane. He should have chats with his crew chief, the line chief and the engineering officer. All are glad to help.

He should learn all about his R/T equipment, and he should plan his conversation for every little situation. He should know about his emergency equipment, Mae West, life raft and jungle kit, keeping all up to date and in 100 per cent working order. All may help him fly another day. He must learn patience.

As the Allied ground situation improved, so did our air equipment, for we changed over to P-47s. This gave us added range, and of course potential altitude advantage. We hated to give up our P-39s, but we were beginning to reach out. Lae had fallen, and Wewak was our target. Here, we ran fighter sweeps and escorted B-24s. We started going over at 25,000 to 30,000 ft (how good it was to know we could look down for a change), but the Japanese never came up. So we came down, and ironically enough, in our first five engagements, in March 1944, we never shot an enemy aircraft down from above 12,000 ft. In fact, we were shooting them down on the deck!

We found we could out-run him on the deck and we knew we could out-dive him, but of course the pull-out and turning factors were still his. But we felt with confidence that we could now meet the enemy on more even terms, and we let our tactics out another notch for more of the sky was ours. The enemy was still a wily opponent, but I felt that his calibre of pilot was deteriorating. When actually engaged and you got on his tail, he seemed resigned to his fate, which he got. But he would try to lure you into his ack-ack, or try to bait you with single 'ducks'. We were not often caught, for lessons had been learned. Although he still had a turning advantage and steeper climb, he chose less and less to fight us.

With our increasing superiority in the air, and our bombers now neutralising the nearer bases, we were forced to reach out further and further with our fighters. Whereas my first two engagements were over Wewak, 250 miles from home, we now began going out 350-450 miles on fighter sweeps. Operating out of Noemfoor, we concentrated on the Vogelkop and Ceram areas. The enemy could not, or would not, come up, so we resorted to dive-bombing and strafing.

It was at this time that our B-24s found a target whose protection warranted stiff Japanese fighter opposition, and the Libs clamoured for cover. Staging from Morotai, and working mostly on carefully planned theories, we flew our new long-range P-47D-28s to Balikpapan, 835 statute miles away. These were offensive sweeps to precede the bombers into the area. Tactics involved going in high (20,000-30,000 ft) and then boiling down into any enemy fighter formations in the air. After a few passes, everyone headed for home. It was pretty much of a ratrace, but the tactics worked for we shot down over 15 enemy aircraft each both times the mission was pulled. Two pilots were missing, one of whom ran short of gas less than two hours from base. History was made for single-engined fighters on these two missions in October 1944.

Shortly after this, operating from Morotai, in the Halmahera, we began 'milk-run' missions with the B-24s and B-25s up to the Philippines. Their job was to neutralise the Negros strips, and the enemy rose to the occasion with unusual vigour for awhile. The 'milk-runs' were 700 miles out to the heart of the enemy island air net! But we had some interesting scraps. The Japanese were usually in the area in strength – up to 30-40 aeroplanes – but they were never in one organised formation.

As close cover, we wanted to give the bombers their protection, but we wanted to make the most of our numbers and opportunities, and work some sort of attrition against Japanese fighter strength. We usually put up 12-16 P-47s to cover a group of B-24s. We adopted tactics which we called 'offensive defence'.

We stayed in relatively close squadron formation, and right on the bombers. When a Japanese fighter (or fighters) was sighted, I immediately started one flight climbing. The remaining flights were then free to chase down any enemy sighted, yet be able to return again and again to the Libs – in other words, don't go too far astray. It was found that the flights off chasing usually scored, while flights with the bombers likewise had fun. The enemy definitely wanted to shoot down our bombers. In one fight, I chased off an initial 'scent', then returned to the bombers in time to see a Japanese aeroplane making a hurried pass on the bombers. I waited on the side, and as he pulled up I sat on his tail and shot him down after a very mild chase.

Returning again to the bombers, I found another Japanese aircraft making a hurried pass – our aggressive area tactics had broken up any organised or leisurely sort of attack. Waiting again on the other side, I found myself on his tail and despatched him too. If gas had permitted, this could have gone on indefinitely. The other flights were keeping the enemy chopped down to size, and although we had only ten P-47s covering 24 B-24s, with 25-30 Japanese fighters in the area, we scored seven kills, two probables and one damaged, and not one bomber was hit. This 'offensive defence' paid dividends as long as the enemy chose to come anywhere close. We fought at altitudes ranging from 5000 to 15,000 ft, and the P-47 really was beautiful.

This concluded my combat. After living on theories and 'dreaming' my fights, when action took place I felt reasonably satisfied. Knowledge, like altitude, was money in the bank. I have always felt that if every man in a formation is doing his job, you will never be jumped, or find yourself in an inextricable defensive position. The old adage of 'the one you don't see gets you' kept my head on a swivel. I demanded, and tried to give, air and radio discipline. I tried to keep learning about my aeroplane, and about new friendly and enemy tactics, etc., even though I was now considered a 'veteran'. As squadron CO, I found that operational accidents were often caused by lack of knowledge of the aeroplane or poor flying habits.

I tried to develop teamwork and cooperation. We never had two-ships shot down, but we lost a few stragglers or wingmen who didn't stick to their job. I learned, and tried to teach, the importance of sun, both for offensive and defensive positioning. I always placed aeroplanes or flights into the sun at a lower level, and those away from the sun were stepped above the leader's flight. We never flew with our backs to the sun. I allowed pilots full freedom to weave when in the target area, because with fewer aeroplanes to work with, it gave us better visual coverage.

Often, a kill is missed by a pilot rushing in before he plans his attack. In my first fight I headed for the nearest enemy aircraft by the shortest route and got only snapshots with nil results. Later, I learned to take a longer course, which, surprisingly, usually led up to the tail of my foe! Then just drive up close, and brother, with those ''fifties'' you can't miss.

49th FIGHTER GROUP

Lt Col Gerald R Johnson
Commanding Officer
49th FG

During my experiences in operating against the Japanese Air Force, there have been evident certain characteristics and traits peculiar to the Japanese as airmen. A knowledge and an understanding of these characteristics is necessary in order to effectively combat the enemy.

First, the quality of the pilots encountered has decreased. It appears that the Japanese Air Force consolidates a group of experienced pilots into a few 'Hot' outfits, instead of spreading these men (and their experience) evenly throughout all its units. One example was the 'Cherry Blossom Hiko-Sentai' which covered the Bismarck Sea Convoy in March 1943.

Maj 'Jerry' Johnson (left) and Capt 'Wally' Jordan had both flown P-39s with the 54th FG in the Aleutians prior to being posted to the 49th FG in April 1943. Firm friends, they served together in the 9th FS, Jordan replacing Johnson as CO of the unit in late January 1944. This photograph was taken at Gusap just prior to Johnson handing command of the unit over to Jordan (*via William Hess*)

Recently, we have engaged a few Japanese fighter pilots who have shown exceptional skill and aggressiveness. The Japanese fighter aeroplanes have all been very manoeuvrable, and when flown by an experienced pilot become a most difficult target to destroy. Fortunately, however, the majority of Japanese pilots encountered are not of this calibre. They are excellent stick and rudder men, but their weakness is that all their manoeuvres are evenly coordinated. They make use of sharp turns and aerobatic manoeuvres, seldom using skids, slips or violent uncoordinated manoeuvres in their evasive tactics. Another characteristic of the younger pilots is their definite lack of alertness. In many recent instances we have engaged enemy fighters and they made no effort to evade our initial attack, evidently because they didn't see us.

Pilots have reported that in addition to being 'surprised', many of the Japanese pilots are either frightened or bewildered once their formation has been split up, and they make little or no effort to evade attack. I have destroyed several fighters recently when they have tried to dive away or make shallow climbing turns. Any one of these pilots could have taken a shot at me if he had utilised his superior manoeuvrability and climb.

In order to effectively attack the enemy, YOU MUST SEE HIM FIRST. If he has an altitude advantage, it is desirable to either climb up to his level or get above him before attacking. You cannot wait to decide what he is going to do – you must plan your attack as you go into action. If your attack is sudden and aggressive, the enemy will be at a disadvantage, regardless of his numbers and position. Do not wait – attack immediately, and pick your targets with the intent to destroy.

We attack as a squadron, but fight in elements of two. The wingman and his element leader are inseparable, and form a most flexible combat team. No matter how the fight progresses, all friendly fighters must remain in the same relative area in order to give each other mutual protection. If a fighter becomes separated from his element, he must join another fighter immediately.

In attacking any Japanese formation, it is essential that you pick out a definite target, then close to effective firing range before cutting loose. Each time you shoot at an enemy aeroplane, observe your errors and correct them in your next attack.

As for identification, we have definitely proven that a pilot isn't within firing range until he can see the roundels on the wings and fuselage of the target aeroplane, and certainly if a pilot can see roundels, he knows that the aeroplane is hostile.

When attacking a superior formation of enemy fighters, we approach at high speed, either on the same level or from above. Our intent is to destroy two or three in the initial attack and scatter their formation. When the enemy formation has been broken, it is possible to pick them off individually. Every effort must be made to reduce the angle of deflection while within firing range. Most kills are made on enemy fighters when the attack is made with less than 20 degrees deflection. Upon meeting a force superior in numbers, it is necessary that everyone attack together. Hit and run is still a most effective tactic if you hit fast and hard.

When attacking an inferior force, we use only the strength necessary, and always maintain a flight or an element as top cover. If we see a single

41

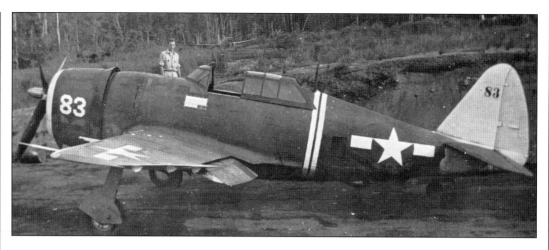

Although hardly a fan of Republic's heavyweight Thunderbolt, 9th FS CO 'Jerry' Johnson nevertheless managed to claim two kills with the fighter soon after the unit swapped its much-loved Lightnings for P-47Ds in November 1943. Johnson primarily flew this particular machine (serial unknown) up until he was posted home on leave on 29 January 1944. Marked up with his command stripes, it is seen here at Gusap whilst in the process of having Johnson's victory tally applied. Note the Vultee Vengeance parked behind the Thunderbolt (*via John Stanaway*)

Japanese aeroplane and suspect a decoy, we send in an element to make the kill, while the remainder of the flight or flights wait for the fighters to dive out of the clouds.

In actual combat the pilot must forget his aeroplane and fly entirely by feel. If he has to be upside down in order to attack an enemy aircraft, then he must shoot from that position. Many inexperienced pilots are hesitant to throw their aeroplane around, but in a fight they must be prepared to execute manoeuvres that they haven't tried before.

When breaking away from an attack, we maintain speed and make a turn away from the target ship. We never fly straight and level during an engagement, and are usually 'split-Sing', climbing or diving all of the time. The reason is that by constantly changing direction, we are never in one position long enough for the hostile pilots to make a successful attack.

SUMMARY OF OFFENSIVE TACTICS

1. Maintain constant alert, see the enemy first and report him to the rest of the flight.

2. Attack as a unit and make your attack sudden and sure.

3. Pick your target and hold your fire until his wingtips protrude beyond the diameter of your ringsight.

4. In attacking an inferior force save your strength for cover.

5. Maintain elements at all costs.

6. Remember – speed and safety are synonymous.

Concerning defensive tactics, here again the pilot must maintain constant vigilance in order to spot the enemy in time to avoid his attack. In the event of an attack by enemy fighters, warn the flight, and at the same time turn sharply into the attackers. The higher their speed, the less chance they have of damaging your aeroplane. Never try to 'dive out' of a

fight – a dive is to be used only to get initial speed. By diving, you remain in the same relative position, except for loss of altitude – you do not remove yourself laterally from the combat area. Always turn sharply into the attacking aeroplane or aeroplanes, then dive enough to obtain a speed of 300-400 mph. Level out in a turn, and if the enemy is still on your tail, skid, slip and change direction continually, maintaining a 500 to 1000 ft/min climb. Soon he will be out of range, and you can smooth out your climb.

If you are attacked by surprise from the rear, the most effective manoeuvre I have ever used is a sharp skidding aileron barrel roll to the right. Throw the wheel or stick hard over with a slight push-over added and let the aeroplane do the rest. You will probably put a crack in the canopy with your head, but you present a most difficult target for the enemy.

Whenever possible, meet the attacking aeroplane with your fire. There are few true head-on passes, and with the concentrated firepower of our fighters, you have a good chance of destroying your opponent.

Should you be leading an element of a flight and attack by hostile fighters is imminent, move out to the side away from the enemy in order that you will have enough room to turn into them and cover your flight leader.

Most important in defence is mutual protection. Always maintain the element, and when engaging the enemy in combat stay in the same general combat area. Sixty per cent of the pilots we lose have become separated from their element or flight. About 25 per cent are killed because they try

Capt Johnson sits in the cockpit of his well-weathered P-38H-1 at Kiriwina Island, awaiting the signal to take off. This shot was taken in October 1943 at the height of the aerial assault on Rabaul. The Fifth Air Force waged an intensive bombing campaign against the Japanese stronghold in New Britain in October and November 1943, and the 49th FG was in the thick of the action escorting medium and heavy bombers. The 9th FS inflicted significant losses on the enemy during these missions, but also suffered heavy attrition to the tune of 16 aircraft destroyed and others damaged – hence the unit's transition onto the P-47 in late November. Johnson claimed six Japanese kills during this period, as well as an Australian Wirraway which he accidentally shot down on 15 November (*via John Stanaway*)

Soon to take command of the 9th FS, Capt Johnson points out one of the names which adorned P-38G-10 42-12882 of 11-kill ace Capt James 'Duckbutt' Watkins. This photograph was taken at Horanda strip in early August 1943 (*via John Stanaway*)

P-38H-1 '83' (serial unknown) was inherited by 'Jerry' Johnson when he replaced Maj Sid Woods as CO of the 9th FS in August 1943. Note the aircraft's old style national markings. It was marked as aircraft '92' when assigned to Woods (*via John Stanaway*)

The first Lightning assigned to 'Jerry' Johnson in the SWPA was P-38F-5 42-12655, which he named *"SOONER"* and had numbered 'white 83'. This machine was written off on 26 July 1943 when its lower left tail section was ripped away by a mortally damaged Ki-61 which Johnson had just hit with cannon and machine gun fire during a head-on attack over Salamaua. Minutes earlier he had claimed his first official kill when he destroyed a Ki-43 over Markham Valley. Johnson struggled back to Horanda Strip, escorted by P-39s from the 39th FS. '83' was subsequently 'scrapped out' (*via John Stanaway*)

to fly AWAY from an attack and do not resort to violent manoeuvring in order to avoid the hostile fire. This may be caused by any number of things, however, as fear and indecision are important factors.

SUMMARY OF DEFENSIVE TACTICS

1. Maintain constant alert.

2. Maintain elements at all costs.

3. Keep speed above 250 mph.

4. Always turn sharply into the attacking aeroplane, except when he is near or dead astern.

5. Use a violent skidding aileron roll if attacked astern from slightly high or low.

6. If the attacking aeroplane is not overrunning you, obtain initial speed by a skidding, diving turn, then begin a 500 to 1000 ft/min climb, using aileron slips and skidding turns to evade fire from the trailing enemy.

Lt Col Johnson (centre, back row) poses with fellow 49th FG HQ pilots at Lingayen soon after he had scored his final kill on 1 April 1945. Flanking the group CO in the back row are Majs George 'Choo-Choo' Laven (four kills) and Clay Tice, whilst in the front row, from left to right, are Capt Bob DeHaven (14 kills), Maj 'Wally' Jordan (six kills) and Capt James 'Duckbutt' Watkins (12 kills). The latter pilot had also claimed his final victory on 1 April 1945. Forming the backdrop to this group shot is 'Jerry' Johnson's last Lightning – an unidentified P-38L-5 which was appropriately named *Jerry*. The fighter boasts his full tally of 25 kills, which included his RAAF Wirraway and two Aleutian 'Rufes' which Johnson always claimed, but which were not officially recognised by the USAAF (*via John Stanaway*)

Gerald R Johnson

Gerald R 'Jerry' Johnson was born on 23 June 1920 in the small town of Kenmore, Ohio. He entered the US Army Aviation Cadet Program in March 1941 and completed his pilot training (almost certainly at Luke Field, in Arizona) on 31 October 1941. The following day he was posted to the 54th Pursuit Group's 57th Pursuit Squadron, which was then equipped with P-40s. In June 1942 the group was hastily despatched to the Aleutian Islands following their invasion by the Japanese. By then the 54th had re-equipped with the P-39, and 'Jerry' Johnson flew a total of 58 combat missions in gales, fog, sleet and snow – these conditions were some of the worst encountered by pilots in World War 2. On 25 September and 1 October he engaged A6M2N 'Rufe' floatplane fighters in the Kiska-Adak area, and months later he was credited with two probable kills by the Fifth Air Force (his controlling body in the Pacific), but not by the Eleventh Air Force, which ran the air war in the Aleutians. The latter claimed that there was no eyewitness evidence of either fighter crashing into the sea.

By October the Japanese forces in the Aleutians had been isolated by a sustained bombing campaign, and with aviators urgently needed in the Pacific, Lt Johnson was among a number of young pilots who transferred back to the United States for conversion training onto the P-38 with the 329th FG's 332nd FS at Glendale, in California. He was posted to the 9th FS/49th FG in April 1943, joining the group at Dobodura, New Guinea. Johnson scored his first confirmed victories over Markham Valley when he downed an 'Oscar' and a 'Tony' on 26 July, and his tally continued to rise during September (when he was also made CO of the 9th FS) and October until, on the 15th of the latter month, he downed an 'Oscar' and two 'Val' dive-bombers whilst defending an Allied invasion force anchored in Oro Bay. He would score a further three kills (a 'Zeke' on 23 October and two more on 2 November) prior to the 9th FS re-equipping with the P-47D. Ironically, Johnson's final Lightning kill of his first tour in the SWPA was an Australian Wirraway, which he shot down in error on 15 November. Fortunately, the light bomber's two-man crew succeeded in baling out unhurt, and a few beers at Dobodura managed to sooth the Australians' 'ruffled feathers'!

The 9th FS had received P-47D-4s in late 1943 due to the attrition the unit had suffered during the large-scale aerial battles over Rabaul in October-November – Lockheed could not supply replacement P-38s quickly enough. Johnson and his pilots despised the large Republic fighter, although the former nevertheless claimed a 'Tony' destroyed on 10 December and a 'Zeke' on 18 January, before returning to the United States for a three-month spell of leave.

This official portrait of a fresh-faced 2Lt 'Jerry' Johnson was taken soon after he had been assigned to the 57th FS/54th FG in the Aleutians in the autumn of 1942 (*via John Stanaway*)

Upon his return to the SWPA, Maj Johnson became deputy commander of the 49th FG, the group having by now totally re-equipped with P-38J/Ls. He scored his next two kills (a Ki-44 'Tojo' and a Ki-43) over Balikpapan, on Borneo, on 14 October, followed by an 'Oscar' and a 'Val' 13 days later during the lead up to the invasion of the Philippines. Johnson would enjoy great success during the Philippines campaign, claiming two 'Zekes' on 11 November over Ormoc Bay and three 'Oscars' and a Ki-49 'Helen' bomber on 7 December off Cebu – he scored the latter victories whilst flying a brand new P-38L-5.

One of those rare individuals who managed to be both a 'hot shot' pilot and a fine administrator, newly-promoted Lt Col 'Jerry' Johnson was made CO of the 49th FG on 10 March 1945, aged just 24. A firm believer in the P-38 as a combat aircraft, his fierce loyalty to the Lockheed fighter was demonstrated at around this time when Johnson was challenged to a mock dogfight by a veteran Mustang pilot from a co-located unit at Lingayen, on Luzon. Determined to teach his 'foe' a lesson, he reportedly added insult to injury by shutting down one of the Lightning's engines and flying formation with the astonished Mustang pilot after Johnson had dominated the aerial engagement!

He claimed his 22nd, and last, kill during a fighter sweep of Hong Kong on 2 April when he downed a solitary Ki-44. Promoted to full colonel in July 1945, Johnson took the 49th FG to Japan for occupation duty following VJ-Day. On 7 October he revealed his courage and bravery one last time. Piloting a B-25, which had been pressed into service by the group as a transport aircraft, Johnson flew into a typhoon whilst trying to reach Tokyo from Ie Shima and became hopelessly lost in the black skies. He ordered everyone to bale out, but one passenger had neglected to bring a parachute. Johnson immediately gave his away, and then tried to fly the B-25 back to base – his co-pilot also elected to stay behind to help him. However, both men were killed when the B-25 crashed during an attempted ditching at sea.

Lt Gen George C Kenney, commander of the Fifth Air Force during World War 2, later told 'Jerry' Johnson's father, 'You are the father of the bravest man I ever knew, and the bravest thing he ever did was the last thing, when he did not need to be brave'.

P-38L-5 44-25463 *Barbara* was yet another late-build Lightning flown by 'Jerry' Johnson in the final months of the war. The fighter was named for his Oregon sweetheart, who became his wife during his extended leave in early 1944 (*via John Stanaway*)

7. Always take definite immediate action when attacked and keep thinking – never give up.

8. Whenever possible, fight back when you are being attacked.

9. Remember that these rules apply for single engine (P-38) operation, as well as for both engines, the only difference being torque and lower speed.

10. You are tougher, more intelligent and have a better team than the Japanese. If you remember that you are not alone, but as a team you are an indestructible force, you will learn that the enemy cannot stand up against your coordinated attacks.

Col George A Walker
Former Commanding Officer
49th FG

Basic formation used is the 16-aeroplane squadron, four-ship flights and two-ship elements. An attempt is always made to have a four-ship flight fight as a unit. This combination has sufficient manoeuvrability and firepower to take care of itself in a fight. However, in a big dogfight the squadron usually ends up in two-ship elements as the fighting teams. It is imperative that they work together and never leave each other.

Dubbed the 'Balikpapan Mob', these men of the 9th FS 'Flying Knights' were amongst the pilots who helped V Fighter Command claim no fewer than 18 kills on 10 October 1944. Photographed at Biak, they are, back row from left to right, Capt Baker (V Fighter Command), Lt Col George Walker (49th FG CO), 2Lt Bob Hamburger, Maj Dick Bong (gunnery instructor), Capt Eddie Howes and 1Lts 'Jimmie' Haislip, Bob Wood, Warren Curton, A Hufford and Carl Estes. In the front row, from left to right, are Majs Robert McComsey (9th FS CO) and 'Wally' Jordan, 1Lt 'Mac' McElroy, Capt 'Wewak Willie' Williams and 1Lt Davis. The Lightning parked behind the pilots is P-38L-5 'black 83', which Maj 'Jerry' Johnson used to down an 'Oscar' and a 'Tojo' during a follow up mission to Balikpapan on 14 October. A colour profile of this machine appears on page 68 (*via John Stanaway*)

This teamwork consists of the wingman flying wide in the attack, which enables him to cross over at anytime for a deflection shot if the element leader cannot get the proper lead. The Japanese fighter, being more manoeuvrable than our aircraft, will turn sharply and attempt to end up on our tail. Thus, as the enemy fighter turns, the wingman positions himself so he gets a deflection shot. The wingman in this combination is as much of a shooter as the element leader. When in a tight spot, the element flies almost abreast and keeps turning toward each other, forming figure eights, each getting head-on passes at any fighter that is on the tail of the other. This method of mutual support is the most satisfactory defence against superior numbers.

Japanese pilots rarely fight as a team, and they break up when attacked. In general, he is a poor shot, and if he loses three or four aircraft at the beginning of a fight, he is prone to decide that it's time to quit.

Individual evasive action in a P-38 is to make a high-speed skidding shallow climb if distance permits. If the attacker is within firing range, a violent uncoordinated manoeuvre is the best. Throwing the wheel into the forward corner with a full aileron roll will result in a skidding three-quarter barrel roll ending up at very high speed, and then climbing at high speed. It is almost impossible to get a lead on an aeroplane in such a manoeuvre, and it has proven very effective in losing the attacker altogether. Another manoeuvre when the attacker is within firing range is to put the aeroplane into a turn, and as soon as you expect fire, throw the aileron hard into the turn, which causes the aeroplane to slide downward, spoiling the attacker's lead until one can get a break to get away.

It is never good to attempt to dive away from a Japanese fighter in a P-38, but as soon as possible get into a high-speed climb or out-run him on the level.

The Japanese fighter pilot's evasion is usually coordinated acrobatics, which enables our pilots to determine deflection lead quite easily. Ours, on the other hand, are always uncoordinated manoeuvres.

MAJ RICHARD I BONG
49th FG

From the experience I have gained in individual combat in this theatre against a number of different types of Japanese fighters and bombers, these facts stand out.

Defence against enemy fighters is resolved around the superior speed of our fighters. If you are jumped from above, dive to pick up an indicated speed of at least 350 mph, then level out and start a shallow climb at high airspeed. Generally speaking, a Japanese fighter will not follow you in a high-speed dive, but occasionally one does, and if this happens, a turn to the right for 90 degrees will throw the enemy pilot behind. The controls stiffen up to excess in high-speed dives, and he cannot follow a sharp diving turn. A turn into the enemy is always effective because they have a healthy respect for the firepower of our aeroplanes. An indicated airspeed never less than 250 mph in combat is good life insurance.

Offensive measures go according to the number of the enemy, but they are always hit and run because a Japanese fighter can out-manoeuvre us

Ranking American ace Capt Dick Bong is the centre of attention for his USAAF colleagues during his war bond tour of the USA in the summer of 1944. Behind him is P-38J-20 44-23481, which was supplied to Bong fresh from Lockheed's Burbank plant. The fighter features the familiar image of Bong's sweetheart, Marge Vattendahl, along with her name in red and white script. Bong's A-2 flying jacket boasts a large 9th FS patch. Note the signatures on the propeller blades (*via John Stanaway*)

about two-to-one. Any number of enemy aircraft can be safely attacked from above. Dive on the group, pick a definite aeroplane as your target and concentrate on him, pull up in a shallow high-speed climb and come bank for another pass. Single enemy aeroplanes or small groups can be surprised from the rear and slightly below a large percentage of the time. He seems to be blind, or he does not look directly behind him enough to spot you, and your first pass should knock him down. Against bombers, it is quite safe to drive right up on the tail of any of them with two exceptions – the 'Betty' and the 'Helen'. These two aeroplanes have a 20 mm cannon which covers a 30-degree arc to the rear, and a beam attack broken off before you reach this cone is the best attack.

It is to be remembered that individual combat as mentioned here is a two-aeroplane element and not a single aeroplane. A two-ship element is our smallest fighting force, and any man by himself is sticking his neck out.

Squadron tactics as I have experienced them are, generally speaking, the same as those of a single element. The leader of a squadron is the commander of the squadron for the period that it is in the air. In a squadron formation, we have 16 aeroplanes in four-ship flights, and two-ship elements within the flights. Number one man in the first flight is the leader. Should he snafu, the lead resolves to the flight leader of the second flight and so on to the flight leader of the fourth flight. The squadron leader's element leader takes over his flight and takes it back to the number two flight position. The number two flight leader moves his flight up and takes over the squadron command.

Control over the squadron is maintained by radio, and the squadron acts as a single unit until the enemy has been engaged. Then each element leader becomes the leader of his unit until the engagement has been broken and squadron formation can again be resumed. It has been found that it is extremely difficult to maintain a squadron formation in any kind of scrap, and so squadron control is broken until the scrap is over.

Squadron defence against enemy fighters is comparatively simple, as enemy fighters will generally not attack if they are seen. However, if they

P-38J-15 42-104012 was the aircraft in which Dick Bong claimed three kills on 12 April 1944 to become the leading US ace (*via William Hess*)

P-38J-15 42-103993 was Dick Bong's mount until another pilot baled out of it in March 1944 when the fighter suffered mechanical failure in bad weather (*via John Stanaway*)

Richard I Bong

Richard Ira 'Dick' Bong was born on 24 September 1920 in Poplar, Wisconsin. Upon graduating from Superior Central High School in 1938, he enrolled as a student at Wisconsin State Teachers' College. Bong never completed his tertiary studies, however, choosing instead to enlist in the Army Reserves on 29 May 1941. He then applied for pilot training, and duly graduated with Class 42-A at Luke Field, Arizona, on 9 January 1942. Bong was considered to be such a gifted flyer that he was kept on at Luke as an instructor for the next three months, before being sent to the 49th FS/14th FG in June after transitioning onto the P-38 at Hamilton Field. He was posted to the 84th FS/78th FG just four weeks later, and seemed destined for the European Theatre of Operations until he was hastily sent to Australia to join the battle-weary 49th FG as an attrition replacement on 14 October 1942.

The group was in the throes of converting its first squadron (the 9th FS) to Lightnings at the time, so Bong, with more P-38 experience than most of his new squadronmates, was sent into combat with

Newly-promoted 1Lt Dick Bong gives his best steely-eyed stare for the camera at Dobodura in this 6 March 1943 shot. Sat in a war-weary P-38F-5, Bong had claimed his sixth kill just three days prior to this photograph being taken (*via William Hess*)

the 17th Provisional Squadron. The latter had been formed to support the hard-pressed 35th FG in New Guinea whilst the 9th FS completed its transition training in Queensland. He duly scored his first two kills (and the first for a 49th FG pilot in a P-38, albeit in a 39th FS/35th FG machine!) on 27 December 1942, when he shot down a 'Zeke' and a 'Val' over Dobodura in P-38F 42-12644. Bong was still flying with the 39th FS when he destroyed three 'Oscars' over Huon Gulf on 7 and 8 January 1943 to 'make ace' (in P-38F-5s 42-124624 and -124653).

He rejoined the 9th FS in late January when the unit moved to Dobodura, and now flying brand new P-38G-5s and G-15s, Bong really began to hit his stride. On 3 March he claimed an 'Oscar', followed by two 'Zekes' eight days later and a 'Doris' (actually a 'Dinah', for the 'Doris' was a fictional type) on the 29th. A solitary 'Betty', downed on 14 April, was his sole success for the next two months, although things picked up again in June and July. Bong got another 'Oscar' on the 12th, and then no fewer than two Ki-43s and two Ki-61s on 26 July over Markham Valley. Two days later another 'Oscar' was added to his scoreboard, raising his tally to 16.

By this time the quiet, young ace was beginning to garner a lot of publicity, Bong becoming an icon in the SWPA. His squadronmates claimed that his P-38 was identifiable in the swirl of battle, and that his presence caused them to take heart. He became an important morale builder within the 49th, being seen as a talisman of indestructibility. Bong himself remained down to earth, shrugging off the attention of both the press and his peers.

October saw him destroy a 'Dinah' on the 2nd and two 'Zekes', over Rabaul, on the 29th. Bong was now flying a P-38H, and on 5 November he again downed two 'Zekes' over Rabaul. Six days later, with his score standing at 20 kills, Bong was sent home on 60 days leave. When he returned to the SWPA in February 1944, he (and fellow ace Lt Col Tommy Lynch, formerly of the 35th FG) was assigned to V Fighter Command Headquarters at Nadzab, rather than a specific squadron. This posting suited Bong perfectly, for he could pick his missions and fly with any unit he wished in an effort to seek out the enemy. The primary reason for this 'special operation' was to ensure that Bong became the first American to pass Eddie Rickenbacker's 26-kill record of World War 1.

Issued with brand new P-38J-15 42-103993, he wasted little time in adding to his tally, claiming a 'Tony' on 11 February, two 'Sally' bombers on 3 March and an 'Oscar' on 3 April. When Bong took off on the morning on 12 April in P-38J-15 42-104012, his score stood at 24 kills. By the time he returned to Nadzab he had boosted his tally to 27, having claimed three 'Oscars' in just a matter of minutes over Hollandia. Having beaten Capt Rickenbacker's 26-year-old record, Bong was immediately promoted to major and sent home on a war bond tour.

He eventually returned to V Fighter Command, ostensibly as a 'Gunnery Training Officer', in the autumn of 1944, and this time he was under strict instructions not to endanger his life in combat. Bong ignored this directive, and by the end of October he had chalked up five more kills. A further three followed in November and four in December, thus taking Bong's score to 40 victories – his final success took the form of a Ki-43, downed on 17 December over Mindoro. Nine days earlier, he had been awarded the Medal of Honor, the decoration being presented to him by Gen Douglas MacArthur. Deemed too valuable to lose in combat, Bong was sent home for good at month-end, having flown an additional 30 missions in his final tour.

Both a press favourite and an exceptional pilot, it was natural that Bong should get involved in the development of Lockheed's latest fighter, the jet-powered P-80 Shooting Star. And it was at the start of yet another routine acceptance flight from Lockheed's Burbank airport on 6 August 1945 that his P-80A-1 (44-85048) suffered an engine flameout on take-off. The fuel-heavy jet crashed into a nearby parking lot and exploded, killing America's ace of aces.

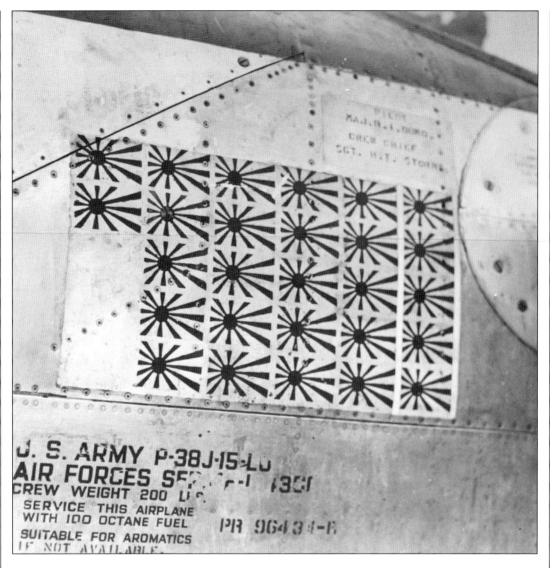

U. S. ARMY P-38J-15-LO
AIR FORCES SE..... .-I I35I
CREW WEIGHT 200 LS.
SERVICE THIS AIRPLANE
WITH 100 OCTANE FUEL   PR 9G4 3 4-E
SUITABLE FOR AROMATICS
IF NOT AVAILABLE.

attack, the formation within the squadron is a defence. The four flights are staggered up and behind, each with about 1000 ft difference in altitude and 2000 ft behind one another. If one of the lower flights is attacked, the top flight can put it off and if the top flight is attacked, it can dive to the side and the lower flights can get on the tail of the attackers. Defence depends chiefly on seeing the enemy before he starts his attack, and some means can be formulated on the spot to avoid it. Look around and you are safe.

Squadron offence works the same way. Depending on the number of enemy aircraft, the squadron leader designates so much high cover to remain up, and the rest of the squadron hit as a unit on the first pass, then resolves itself into combat elements until the Japanese have been shot or dispersed.

Enemy bomber formations will be taken on the same way, with part of the squadron attacking the escorting fighters and the rest attacking the bombers as directed.

P-38J-15 42-104380 was yet another Lightning flown by Dick Bong in the SWPA in 1944. This machine bears 27 victory symbols, denoting its assignment to him soon after he broke Rickenbacker's World War 1 scoring record. Rumour has it that this particular aircraft may have also been flown on occasion by legendary aviator Charles Lindbergh during his lengthy tour of V Fighter Command units in the SWPA in 1944 (*via John Stanaway*)

CAPT ROBERT M DEHAVEN
7th FS/49th FG

It has been firmly established that in the P-40, the best individual defensive manoeuvre is the 'split-S' if the attack is in progress – that is if we have been jumped. The ability to roll a P-40 on its back and gain speed quickly straight down is usually sufficient to evade the fire of the enemy. We have found this manoeuvre to be effective as low as 5000 ft. However, in the dive we adhere to the ironclad rule of never pulling out in the same direction that we go in. Even a half roll is enough to disrupt the enemy fire and confuse him as to our direction of pull-out. In the case of the Type 3 'Tony' fighter, that statement must be qualified to the extent that one must have altitude to dive away. The 'Tony' will dive with our aeroplanes up to speeds of 400 mph, but it is apparently allergic to high-speed pull-outs, and we have 'shaken' it in that manner.

We have also, on occasion, used the push-over when jumped by the 'Oscar' or 'Zeke' because their carburation system will not feed their radial engines on a sudden push-over. However, a steep dive is difficult to attain in this fashion, and the danger of 'redding out' makes it more detrimental than beneficial. On top of that, while our aeroplane is gaining speed slowly, the enemy may half-roll and be in an easy position to shoot.

In the event that the enemy is seen starting the attack, it has been our policy to wait until he commits himself definitely as to direction and then turn into him. The Japanese pilot is generally not overeager for a head-on pass, and a sudden turn into him will usually delay his attack long enough for us to get out of gun range and gain altitude using a high-speed climb. It has been our experience in combat and against captured Japanese enemy aircraft that with a slight distance advantage, a shallow high-speed climb will pull us away from the 'Tony', 'Oscar' or 'Zeke'.

In case the enemy is above us, but has not yet committed himself to attack, our practice has been to get out from under, gain altitude keeping him in sight and then return to make our own passes. Peculiarly, we have found that the enemy is not likely to follow us either singly or in groups while we are in the process of pulling away and gaining altitude. We have found that with an initial altitude 2000 ft greater than that of the enemy, on many occasions four passes can be made before we are forced to leave the fight and regain altitude.

The last of the individual defensive manoeuvres concerns being caught on the deck, and, needless to say, that's a tough spot to be in. If you are alone and the enemy is diving for the attack, his speed is too great for us to try pulling away. Therefore, the only alternative is to put your foot on the throttle, turn into him and/or skid the aeroplane violently. If he is behind and in gun range, pushing and pulling the stick to get a roller coaster effect has often worked safely, but other than that, a 'firewalled' throttle quadrant and a violent skid are the only choices we have. About that time, a prayer comes in handy too.

The old adage 'safety in numbers' probably applies better on squadron defence than anywhere else. The teamwork must be at its peak in order to keep a fighting unit efficient while under attack. Naturally, the formation a squadron flies is basically defensive at all times, and we have found the best method is to have the flights stacked up and approximately 800 ft apart. Horizontally, they are staggered to the right and left of the lead flight, and are constantly, but smoothly, using their flexibility to gain a maximum of visibility and freedom of movement.

Unfortunately, the Japanese are extremely reluctant to attack full squadron of fighters. We have had them attack the top one or two flights, in which cases we tried to bring the enemy down into the bottom flights. If this did not succeed, we tried to maintain a 'scissoring' manoeuvre with the elements or with the flights, diving out and sacrificing altitude as a last resort. Which brings up the basis of squadron defensive tactics. We stress

Robert M DeHaven

Robert Marshall DeHaven was born on 13 January 1922 in San Diego, California. He enrolled in the Washington and Lee University in the late 1930s, but left prior to graduation in order to join the Army Reserves in February 1942. Earning his wings with Class 43-A at Luke Field, Arizona, on 4 January 1943, DeHaven transitioned onto the P-40 in Florida and was then sent to the Hawaii-based 73rd FS/318th FG. Units in action in the SWPA were desperately short of qualified pilots at this time, and DeHaven was duly transferred to V Fighter Command's 7th FS/49th FG in May 1943. Travelling firstly to Australia and then to New Guinea, the future ace eventually arrived at the unit's Dobodura, base after several weeks of travel.

The by now well-travelled DeHaven claimed his first kill on 14 July (in P-40K-1 42-45985) when he downed a 'Val' dive-bomber over Salamaua. Further successes followed in October, when he destroyed an 'Oscar' on the 17th and a 'Zeke' and a 'Tony' ten days later (all in P-40N-5 42-104957). DeHaven 'made ace' on 10 December with the destruction of a 'Tony' in P-40N-5 42-105405, and two days later another Ki-43 fell to his guns – both kills were claimed near Alexishafen. The New Year started well for DeHaven, with a Ki-61 destroyed on 2 January and an 'Oscar' on the 23rd of the month. Another Ki-43 was downed on 15 March. He claimed a rare D4Y 'Judy' dive-bomber as his tenth, and last, P-40 victory on 7 May, although he was not totally sure of the aircraft's type. What was not open to speculation, however, was DeHaven's tally with the Warhawk, his ten kills making him equal top scorer (with Capt Ernest A Harris of the 8th FS/49th FG) on the type in V Fighter Command.

There was little opportunity for DeHaven to add to his tally during the summer of 1944, his squadron at last transitioning to the P-38 during this period, and the 49th FG as a whole making ready for the recapture of the Philippines in the autumn. DeHaven's first Lightning score came on 29 October when he destroyed an 'Oscar' over Biliran Island, and his final trio of victories swiftly followed on 1, 2 and 4 November, when he claimed two 'Zekes' and a J2M 'Jack' fighter whilst patrolling over Leyte. Boosting his final tally to 14 kills, DeHaven was then sent home on leave. He returned to the 49th FG as group operations officer in 1945, but failed to add to his score prior

and impress the importance of the two-ship element. From that stems the cardinal rule of combat – NEVER FIGHT ALONE. That two-ship element is not only protection, it is a potent striking force. If jumped, and the attack is expected, or if caught on the deck, two aeroplanes in constant movement covering one another have a 100 per cent better chance of getting away.

Inside the flights, the wingmen are flown well up and well out so everyone is covering behind and above everyone else. In case number four man is attacked, he is up far enough so that the element leader can turn

to VJ Day. By war's end DeHaven, who was the 7th FS's ranking ace, had flown 272 combat missions.

Choosing to leave the Army Air Force post-war, DeHaven did not completely sever his lengths with the military, however, for he joined the California Air National Guard and acted as its P-80 acceptance test pilot. He transferred to the Air Force Reserve in 1950, from which he retired with the rank of colonel in 1965. In civilian life, DeHaven found employment with Hughes Aircraft Company in 1948, where he worked as an engineering test pilot and personal pilot to Howard Hughes. He eventually became an executive of the company and manager of the flight test division for over 30 years. During that time DeHaven was elected a Fellow in the Society of Experimental Test Pilots and also served as President of the American Fighter Aces Association. He currently resides in Encino, California.

Joint top-scoring P-40 pilot in V Fighter Command, Bob DeHaven continued his run of successes in combat when his unit transitioned onto the P-38L in the late summer of 1944 (*via William Hess*)

into the attacker, either head-on or front quarter. The same holds true for the elements which are able to turn into one another for mutual support.

Inasmuch as no two combats are identical, it is difficult to make any set rules governing an attack. The only definite advantages we always try to gain are altitude, speed and position. In the case of fighters, we naturally like to originate our attacks from above and behind, or in the sun. Due to the 'flying circus' formation the enemy usually flies, the element of surprise is eliminated. However, being above gives us opportunity to gain superior speed, make a pass to break up their group and then pull back up to altitude.

When attacking groups of two, three or four enemy aircraft by oneself, it's safe to say that they will attempt to 'box in' the individual.

One favourite manoeuvre by three Zeros is the 'Prince of Wales', in which the leader does a loop and the wingmen make opposite chandelles. To follow any one is to invite the other two for 'Bingo', therefore, so we usually take a snapshot at one, keep going, regain altitude and try again. In the case of two or four, they will usually be spread out and stacked up. If the opportunity is such that we can hit the top man, we do so, but attempting to attack low men, even with superior speed, is not conducive to a safe trip home. Of late, we have found enemy pilots who will take a head-on pass, and with our greater firepower it's usually disastrous for them. They do, however, have the trick of coming in head-on, rolling and firing on their backs. Then as they pass under, they execute a 'split-S' and loop up under

Capt DeHaven poses with his elaborately marked P-38L (serial unknown) at Lingayen in June 1945. All of his aircraft were marked with the number 13, this particular machine being DeHaven's mount during his brief second tour in the SWPA in mid 1945. Note the dive-bombing guides in the form of black stripes marked on the wing leading edge inboard of the port engine (*via John Stanaway*)

us. This is readily counteracted by making a tight chandelle as soon as they roll and pass underneath. In one-against-one fights, a Japanese pilot who knows his aircraft can, and did, make a fool of one P-40 by continuous tight turns into the attack. In such circumstances it is best to bring in another aeroplane, or let the enemy go before he has a chance to reverse the advantage.

In squadron attack on fighters, the cornerstone of teamwork is the element. Once a fight has started, the situations change too suddenly and too rapidly to keep 16 ships – and usually even four – together. When attacking fighters, we use the same tactics described before – position, altitude and speed. After the first attack, the enemy is broken up, and naturally to destroy him we must separate. However, there have been occasions when only six or eight enemy were sighted below us, and then the squadron control was of primary importance. Without exception, against small numbers two flights are instructed to maintain a high cover, while two flights engage the enemy. If he succeeds in climbing away, the top flights are there to engage, and likewise enemy fighters coming down are intercepted. This same type of cover is used when strafing or dive-bombing, keeping at least four ships high at all times.

When escorting bombers – usually close cover – our primary purpose is to protect them and not to force a fight, unless specifically instructed to do so. When it is obvious that the enemy will attempt to intercept the bombers, the flights spread out to more or less the four sides. In this type of interception, almost always we have our altitude advantage which we try to keep up, going down to shoot off the enemy, then pulling back up to the bombers. If, in turn, we have no high cover, the flights are deployed so that at least one flight will remain above the enemy.

On the interception of enemy bombers, we have found we can always count on fighters above them. In such a case, the squadron leader designates two flights to go high into the fighters, while two hit the bombers. The best attack is considered low front quarters. We try to coordinate our attacks and plan according to the size of the bomber formation. If small, an element pass is best. If large, a flight pass in nearly line abreast is most effective. If dive-bombers, we usually use a string formation.

In the matter of coordinating, two ships will go in from the right front quarter and two from the left, dispersing the enemy fire by hitting from the two directions at once. Two aeroplanes will go over the bombers and break down and out, and the other two will go under and break the same way. If enemy fighters break through to attack us, we try to make our passes regardless, sucking them in where they will chance hitting their own bombers and vice versa. Whenever the bombers are turned back or the sky is clear of the enemy, we always try to rejoin with at least one other person, or a complete flight, in case of interception on the way home.

MAJ WALLACE R JORDAN
9th FS/49th FG

Primarily, one principle which underlies the successful application of all the following fighter-to-fighter combat tactics with the Japanese is the neutralisation of the excellent manoeuvrability of his aeroplane. In my

Wallace R Jordan

Wallace Robert 'Wally' Jordan was born on 22 October 1916 in San Francisco, California. Joining the Army Reserves, he commenced flying training as an aviation cadet on 23 April 1941 and received his wings just four days after the surprise attack on Pearl Harbor – his was the first class to graduate from advanced flying training following the raid. Transitioning onto the P-40 and then the P-39, Jordan was eventually sent to the Aleutians in 1942 to serve with the Airacobra-equipped 54th FG. Here, he battled the enemy and the weather whilst escorting B-24s on bombing raids against Japanese bases on Kiska Island.

Like his good friend 'Jerry' Johnson, 'Wally' Jordan returned to the United States in January 1943 and converted onto the P-38 with the 329th FG at Glendale, in California. In April, he and Johnson were assigned to the 9th FS/49th FG, which was flying P-38s from Dobodura, in New Guinea. Promoted to captain on 26 July, Jordan scored his first victory exactly one week later when he downed an 'Oscar' south of Saidor. In November the 9th FS was equipped with P-47Ds, which it retained until March 1944. Few victories were claimed in this period, as the unit's pilots lacked confidence in the big Republic fighter. However, proving his ability to fly virtually any aircraft well, Jordan downed a Ki-43 on 14 March 1944 – just days prior to the unit's conversion back onto the P-38J. By then he was CO of the 9th FS, having replaced his friend 'Jerry' Johnson, who had gone on leave on 29 January. The latter had requested that Jordan, who he rated as an 'ice man' in combat, take over 'his' unit while he was in the United States.

Maj 'Wally' Jordan obscures the serial of his P-38L-5 with a strategically placed hand in this portrait, taken at Biak in October 1944. Note the metal case for his sunglasses tucked into the belt of his flying overall (*via William Hess*)

Promoted to major on 18 April, Jordan was involved in a jeep accident shortly afterwards, which left him with a visible scar on his head and the nickname 'Major Stitch'! Later that same month he joined the 49th FG's staff, and scored his third victory when he shot down a 'Tojo' on 19 May. Jordan did not score again until 10 October, when the group undertook the longest fighter escort mission ever flown up to that point in the war in support of bombers sent to attack oil targets at Balikpapan, on Borneo. Flying a new P-38L-1, he destroyed a Ki-45 'Irving' twin-engined fighter and an 'Oscar' near the target area, thus gaining ace status. Four days later he claimed his final kill, again over Balikpapan, when he downed yet another Ki-43 (he also claimed a second 'Oscar' as a probable on this date).

'Wally' Jordan transferred to the Regular Army on 5 July 1946 and later to the Air Force upon its formation. Promoted to full colonel on 1 June 1952, he eventually retired in 1964.

experience, manoeuvrability is the only quality in which the enemy excels, and when allowed, he will use it to its fullest extent, The neutralisation is effected simply by fighting in a manner that does not allow him to use his manoeuvrability.

INDIVIDUAL DEFENSIVE TACTICS

First, do not attempt to dogfight. If you do, your chances are minimised by allowing the enemy to use manoeuvrability.

When enemy contact is imminent – i.e. over a target – maintain an IAS of at least 250 mph. From this speed, increased settings will quickly give you the necessary high speed when needed.

Upon being attacked, several things can be done according to the type of attack. If seriously outnumbered, and attacked from above, establish a shallow dive at War Emergency setting until out of danger. If attacked from below, use a high-speed shallow climb. The enemy climbs more vertically and cannot stay with you in this type of climb.

If attacked by a single enemy, allow him to commit himself in his pass – turn sharply in and under at the critical moment. A great many times you will be able to get a short head-on shot in this situation. Maintain this turn through the shortest possible period. Get out far enough to regain altitude and return offensively.

Recently, with the use of the dive flaps and aileron boost on the L-series P-38, the following defensive manoeuvre has been very successful. 'Split-S', roll 180 degrees while going straight down and pull out. This manoeuvre was used by a pilot in the squadron at 3000 ft altitude. Low, it should be used only as a last resort, since it allows the enemy to use his manoeuvrability if he so desires, and is good enough to follow. High, it can be used to better advantage, since you will be able to hold straight down after the 180-degree straight down roll, building up excessive speed to where the attacker cannot stay with you. This manoeuvre and the normal 'split-S' should not be used unless absolutely necessary, because the consequent loss of altitude is to your general disadvantage.

At any time, your best individual defensive action is to rejoin another friendly aeroplane and use the teamwork of the two-ship element for your mutual protection.

INDIVIDUAL OFFENSIVE TACTICS

When individually attacking an enemy fighter, use the speed necessary to prevent over-running, come from sun or cloud cover, and do not fire until minimum range is reached unless the enemy aircraft starts evasive action before that time. With premature firing, your ammunition is wasted by your tracers, prompting the enemy to evasive action that you cannot possibly follow. The best pass, if you can get set for it, is to come in directly behind and slightly low. From this position, you can close to minimum range, pull up to level altitude with the enemy and destroy him before he realises you are there.

The majority of Japanese pilots dislike the head-on pass and will not press it to minimum. If one does, your superior firepower will give you a distinct advantage.

If attacking superior numbers, pick the most vulnerable target, make a straight pass with plenty of speed and keep on going. In this instance, if you turn more than 45 degrees, you will usually be immediately and seriously on the defensive.

The evasive manoeuvres favoured by the enemy are 'split-S', Immelmans, tight loops, steep diving turns and chandelles. I have seen the double Immelman used occasionally. The enemy does this difficult manoeuvre with amazing ease. Most of these turns will be made to the left. Usually, they are executed so quickly, and the radii of the turns so short, that you cannot follow. Bide your time, keep altitude and make another pass. If you try to follow, the tight loop or a reversal from any of the enemy's tight turns can easily put him on your tail.

If you anticipate fighting the Japanese, be especially proficient in deflection shooting, because the majority of your shots fired in anger will be that type.

SQUADRON DEFENSIVE TACTICS

The squadron formation, both offensive end defensive, is based upon, and expands from, the two-ship element. The flights are four-ship, consisting of two two-ship elements. Within the flight, the wingman of the flight leader and the element fly wide, almost abreast on opposite sides of the flight leader. The wingman crosses under and the second element over. As much of the time as is possible, the second element is flown high, with the first element between the second and the sun. This makes for easier handling of attacks from the sun. Close checking upon element leaders is sometimes necessary to see that this is done, since some may thoughtlessly fly the more comfortable sunward side.

The squadron formation, if each flight is considered as a single aeroplane, looks relatively the same as a flight when viewed from above. There is an average depth, stepped up from the lead flight, of 1000 ft. These positions afford maximum visibility, flexibility and ease to hold. From them, maximum firepower can quickly be brought to bear on an attack from any direction. We insist upon close show formation around home base before and after missions. This increases alertness of the pilots for all formation flying.

In instances where it is impossible to get away otherwise, flights or elements who are outnumbered and cannot fire – out of ammunition etc. – can usually force the enemy to break off by making bluff passes. This has been done successfully a number of times. Recently, Lt Helterline, out of ammunition, made bluff passes on three enemy fighters which were attacking an aeroplane with only a single operable engine. They broke off and the single engine returned safely.

Upon completion of a fight, squadron formation must be resumed as quickly as possible in order to conserve gas and to protect any cripples.

SQUADRON OFFENSIVE TACTICS

When we are offensive to start, we strive to maintain the flight formation, but do not insist upon it, since keeping a flight together in the general melee of a fight is very difficult. We do, however, insist that the wingman stay in and keep the two-ship element intact. There will be a few instances where even this will not be possible. If a break up of two-ship elements occurs, the singles must rejoin another friendly fighter as soon as possible, and where possible, elements rejoin to form flights.

A 9th FS photo-call at Tacloban in late October 1944, just days after the unit had flown into the newly-liberated airfield. Aces Jordan, Bong and Johnson stand side-by-side immediately below the nose of P-38L-1 44-23964, which had been Bong's mount during his attachment to the 49th FG as 'gunnery instructor' throughout the Philippines campaign. The ace would claim six kills with the fighter between 10 October and 11 November 1944, taking his score to 36 victories. 44-23964 was subsequently lost whilst being flown by 49th FG Deputy Ops Officer Maj John Davis on 28 November, the pilot perishing when the fighter stalled in soon after taking off from Tacloban. A colour profile of this aircraft appears on page 70 (*via John Stanaway*)

When an enemy formation is sighted, the squadron or flight leader immediately calls in the clock position of enemy aircraft, and if they are higher, attains an altitude necessary to attack. At this time the flights must space themselves far enough to avoid following the leader's flight too closely, thus having time to pick a good target, make an effective pass and avoid collisions with enemy or friendly aircraft.

Once the initial pass has been made and the enemy formation has been dispersed, it is the job of the various two-ship elements to mop up the remaining Japanese aircraft. Pilots must be indoctrinated to restrain their eagerness to shoot where several are trying to get in a pass. If they all press in at once, none will get a shot and collisions will be imminent. If two or more are attacking (this applies especially where there are several trying to get one aircraft), the formation should spread very wide and allow one man to attack. If this is done, the enemy's evasive move will usually carry him within range of another member of the formation.

Another aspect of this case is concerned with hot guns and the resultant swirling of rounds therefrom. After any amount of sustained shooting, your guns need at least ten minutes of cooling. If they are not given this cooling, the rounds will swirl, go in every direction and you will hit nothing. When the swirl is observed, pull off and allow someone else to take over the attack until your guns have returned to normal. Actually, your guns won't get the chance to overheat if you coordinate properly with the rest of the flight or element, because the target's evasive actions will change his attacker frequently. Recently, we had an enemy aircraft get away from a flight of six P-38s simply because all members, thinking of their own personal score of course, shot at once, got in each other's way and at the end couldn't hit anything with overheated guns.

Intelligence Officers must continually brief pilots as to enemy order of battle, types likely to be encountered and all information concerning them – mainly speeds – because they are necessary to compute lead in the oft-encountered deflection shot.

LONG REACH

All the foregoing information applies fundamentally to the tactics of long reach. The differences will occur in the formation to and from the target. We use 1600 RPM and the necessary manifold pressure setting to maintain 185 mph IAS, which is the computed most efficient airspeed for minimum fuel consumption where the aeroplane carries two external tanks. The speed without external tanks is 175 mph. These figures were given to us by Charles Lindbergh and, since we have no other source of information, we have taken them to be correct. Actually, we have never had to cut the IAS back that far on return. Without external tanks, 24 inches and 1600 RPM will give an IAS of 200 mph at 10,000 ft.

In order to reduce drag, the external tanks are burned out separately and dropped when empty. Most aeroplanes will give two hours, or slightly better, with a climb included. If the mission is not over 800 miles, the second tank will last to the target plus 15 minutes. The last 15 minutes are at high settings since you are over the target, so we assume that we could probably reach 900 miles on the external wing tanks.

The accomplishment of long radius of action (over 300 miles) is based upon the following – use of eight-ship section, which I will explain in the next paragraph, no interception en route, an advanced rendezvous point and good weather. An advance fighter sweep is not essential, but is preferable.

On a mission where the radius is over 800 miles, we split the squadron and go on course as eight-ship sections, which take off and go on course immediately. The leader will make a turn of not more than 180 degrees after take off, assembling loosely and going on course without waiting for the second eight. A squadron assembly over the field, and maintenance of it to the rendezvous, will result in the use of too much fuel. Obviously, this condition prevails only where one strip suitable to take off one aeroplane at a time is available – for example, Morotai during the Borneo missions. With proper on-the-ball assembly, a full squadron can perform the mission, but would have a very small fighting and weather reserve.

At low settings, the changes in speed of the aeroplane are very sluggish. Increase of manifold pressure at the excessively low RPM has very little effect upon increasing the speed of the aeroplane. However, increase of RPM to the necessary amount has the desired effect. For this reason, all pilots use RPM to maintain formation on the longer missions.

The type of formation flown is identical to normal combat type except that it is flown much more loosely. This prevents jockeying of settings and consequent use of extra fuel. The formation is not so loosely flown that aircraft are outside supporting distance of one another,

These are fighter tactics as we know and use them. Having only recently become a full P-38 group, our squadron tactics may change somewhat to accommodate operations where the group flies as a unit. However, we do not anticipate any important fundamental change.

COLOUR PLATES

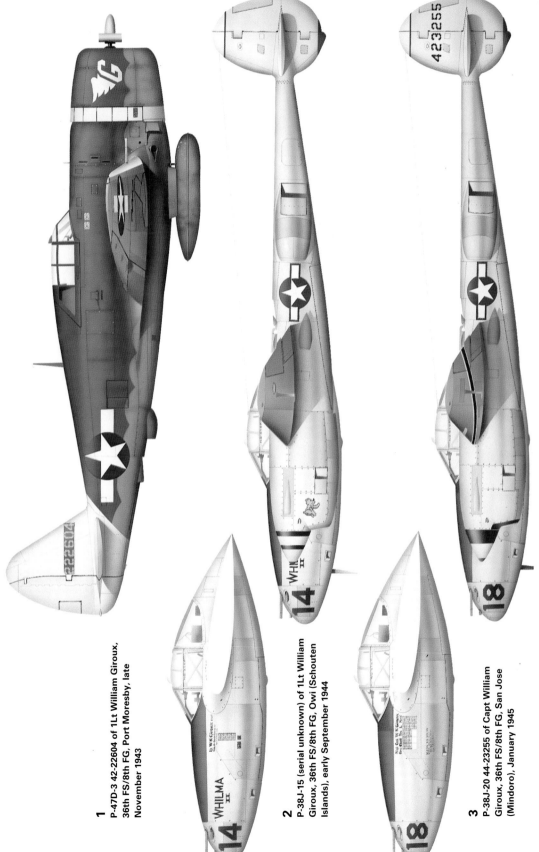

1
P-47D-3 42-22604 of 1Lt William Giroux, 36th FS/8th FG, Port Moresby, late November 1943

2
P-38J-15 (serial unknown) of 1Lt William Giroux, 36th FS/8th FG, Owi (Schouten Islands), early September 1944

3
P-38J-20 44-23255 of Capt William Giroux, 36th FS/8th FG, San Jose (Mindoro), January 1945

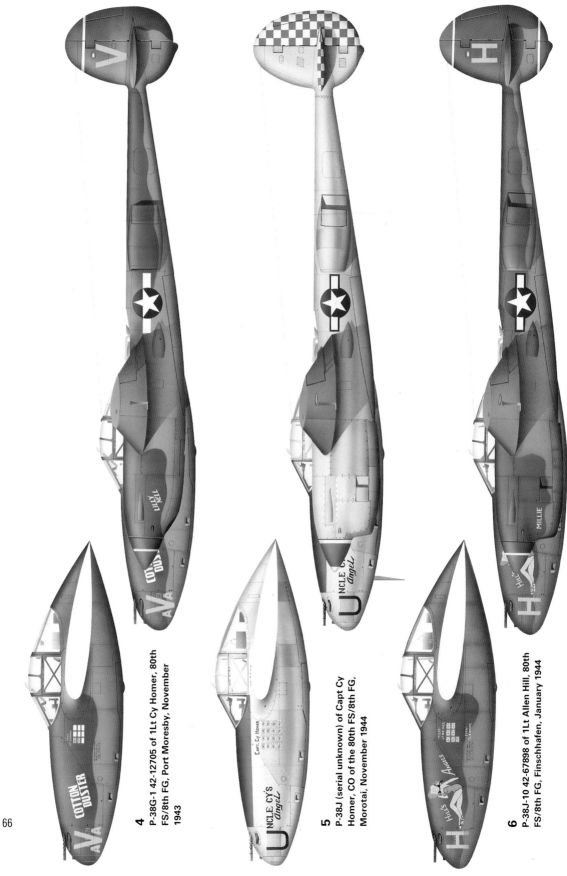

4
P-38G-1 42-12705 of 1Lt Cy Homer, 80th FS/8th FG, Port Moresby, November 1943

5
P-38J (serial unknown) of Capt Cy Homer, CO of the 80th FS/8th FG, Morotai, November 1944

6
P-38J-10 42-67898 of 1Lt Allen Hill, 80th FS/8th FG, Finschhafen, January 1944

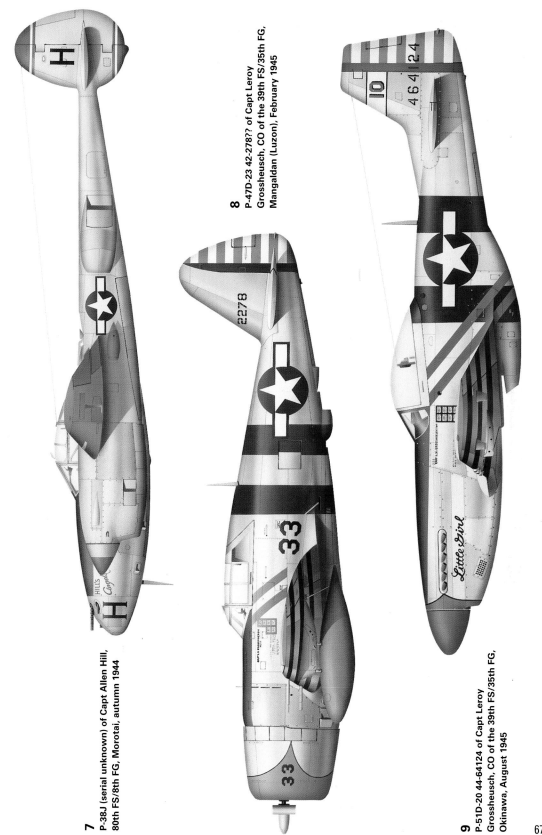

7
P-38J (serial unknown) of Capt Allen Hill,
80th FS/8th FG, Morotai, autumn 1944

8
P-47D-23 42-2787? of Capt Leroy
Grossheusch, CO of the 39th FS/35th FG,
Mangaldan (Luzon), February 1945

9
P-51D-20 44-64124 of Capt Leroy
Grossheusch, CO of the 39th FS/35th FG,
Okinawa, August 1945

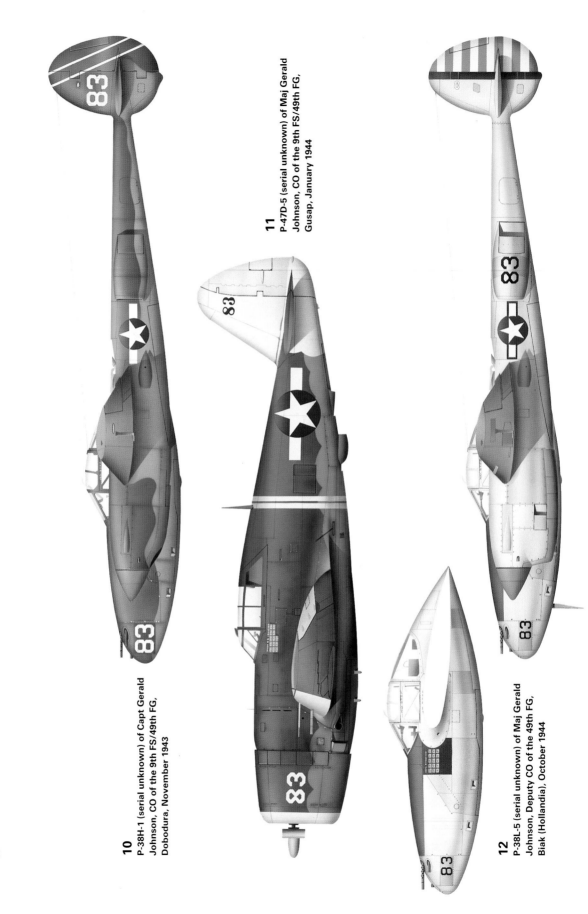

10
P-38H-1 (serial unknown) of Capt Gerald Johnson, CO of the 9th FS/49th FG, Dobodura, November 1943

11
P-47D-5 (serial unknown) of Maj Gerald Johnson, CO of the 9th FS/49th FG, Gusap, January 1944

12
P-38L-5 (serial unknown) of Maj Gerald Johnson, Deputy CO of the 49th FG, Biak (Hollandia), October 1944

13
P-40N-5 42-105826 of Maj Gerald
Johnson, 49th FG HQ, Biak (Hollandia),
October 1944

14
P-38G-5 (serial unknown) of 1Lt Dick
Bong, 9th FS/49th FG, Dobodura, July
1943

15
P-38J-15 42-103993 of Capt Dick Bong,
V Fighter Command, Gusap, March
1944

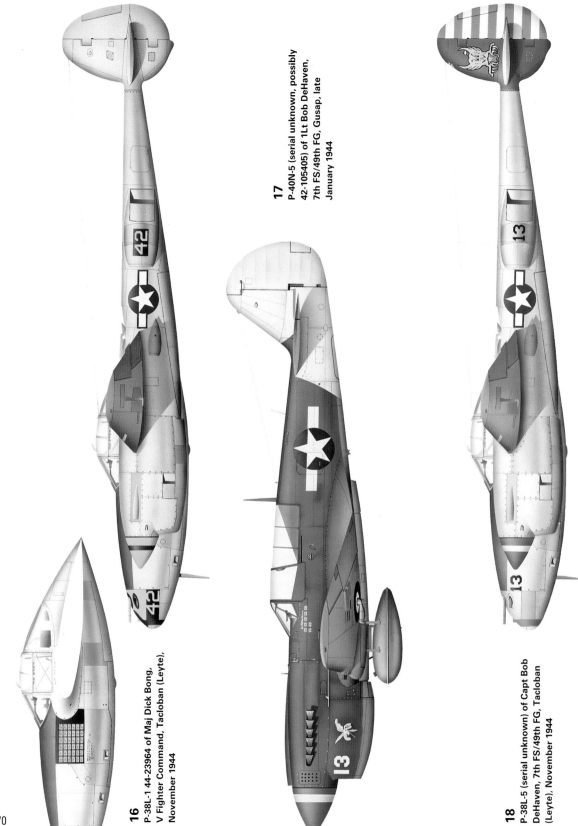

16
P-38L-1 44-23964 of Maj Dick Bong,
V Fighter Command, Tacloban (Leyte),
November 1944

17
P-40N-5 (serial unknown, possibly
42-105405) of 1Lt Bob DeHaven,
7th FS/49th FG, Gusap, late
January 1944

18
P-38L-5 (serial unknown) of Capt Bob
DeHaven, 7th FS/49th FG, Tacloban
(Leyte), November 1944

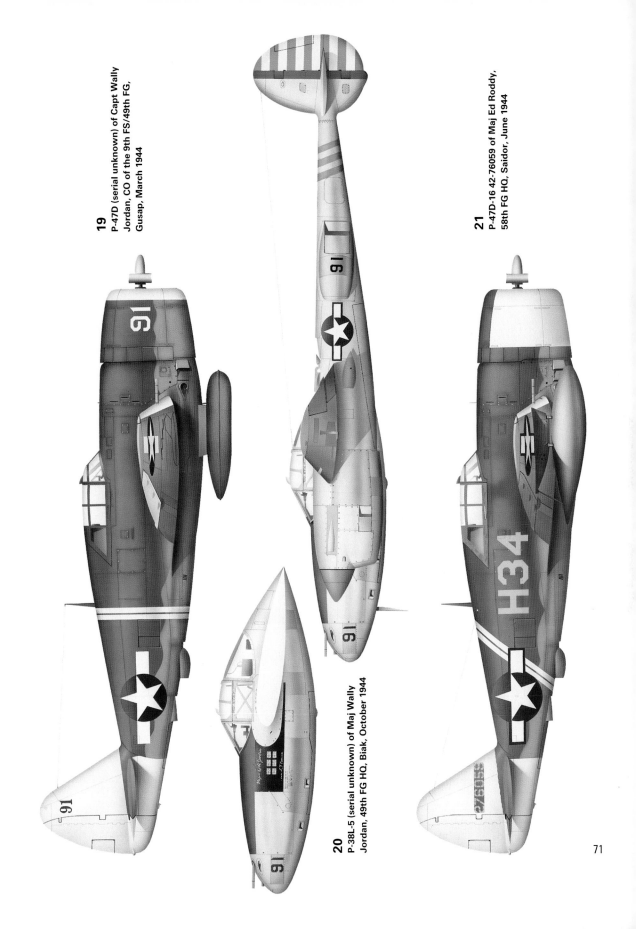

19
P-47D (serial unknown) of Capt Wally
Jordan, CO of the 9th FS/49th FG,
Gusap, March 1944

21
P-47D-16 42-76059 of Maj Ed Roddy,
58th FG HQ, Saidor, June 1944

20
P-38L-5 (serial unknown) of Maj Wally
Jordan, 49th FG HQ, Biak, October 1944

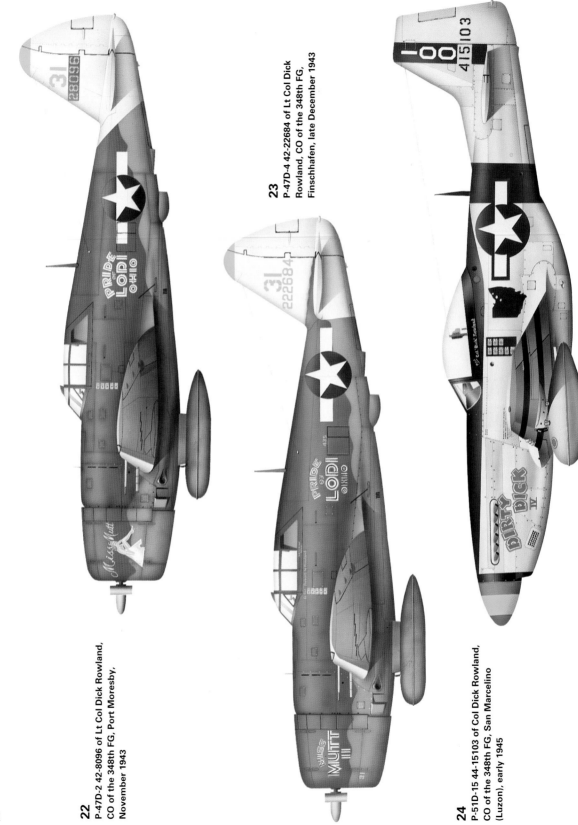

22
P-47D-2 42-8096 of Lt Col Dick Rowland,
CO of the 348th FG, Port Moresby,
November 1943

23
P-47D-4 42-22684 of Lt Col Dick
Rowland, CO of the 348th FG,
Finschhafen, late December 1943

24
P-51D-15 44-15103 of Col Dick Rowland,
CO of the 348th FG, San Marcelino
(Luzon), early 1945

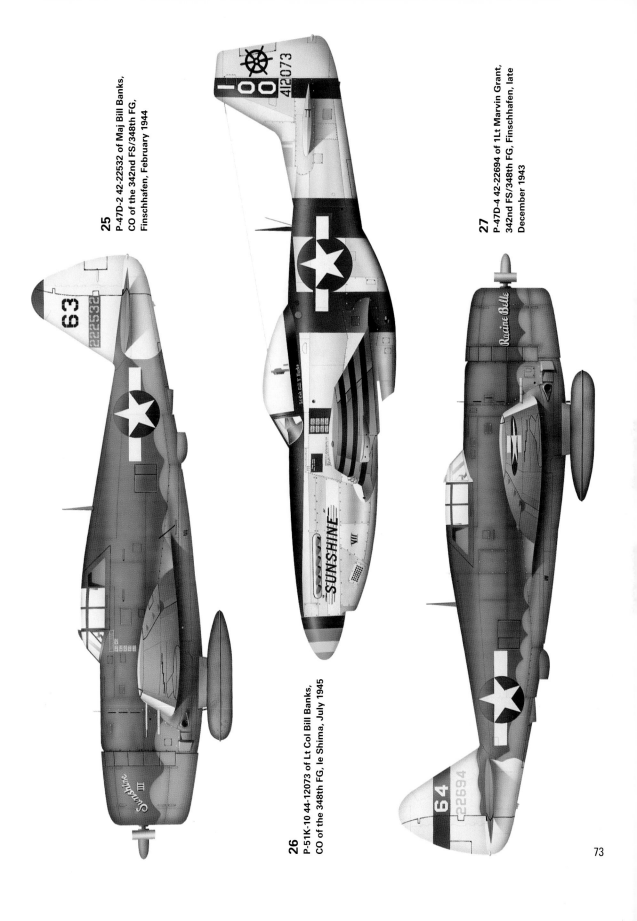

25
P-47D-2 42-22532 of Maj Bill Banks,
CO of the 342nd FS/348th FG,
Finschhafen, February 1944

26
P-51K-10 44-12073 of Lt Col Bill Banks,
CO of the 348th FG, Ie Shima, July 1945

27
P-47D-4 42-22694 of 1Lt Marvin Grant,
342nd FS/348th FG, Finschhafen, late
December 1943

28
P-47D-23 42-27886 of Capt Marvin Grant,
342nd FS/348th FG, Leyte, November
1944

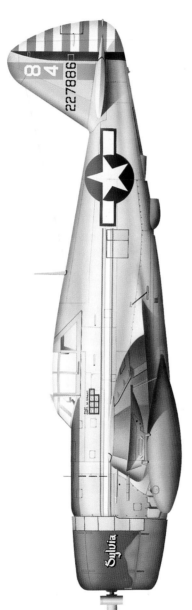

29
P-47D-23 42-27884 of Maj Bill Dunham,
CO of the 460th FS/348th FG, Leyte,
December 1944

30
P-51K-10 44-12017 of Lt Col Bill Dunham,
Deputy CO of the 348th FG, Ie Shima,
August 1945

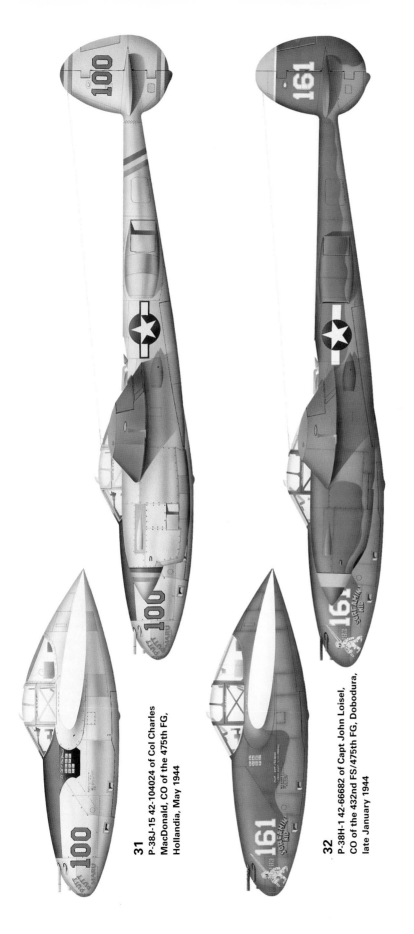

31
P-38J-15 42-104024 of Col Charles
MacDonald, CO of the 475th FG,
Hollandia, May 1944

32
P-38H-1 42-66682 of Capt John Loisel,
CO of the 432nd FS/475th FG, Dobodura,
late January 1944

33
P-38L-5 44-25643 of Maj John Loisel,
475th FG HQ, Dulag (Leyte), late January
1945

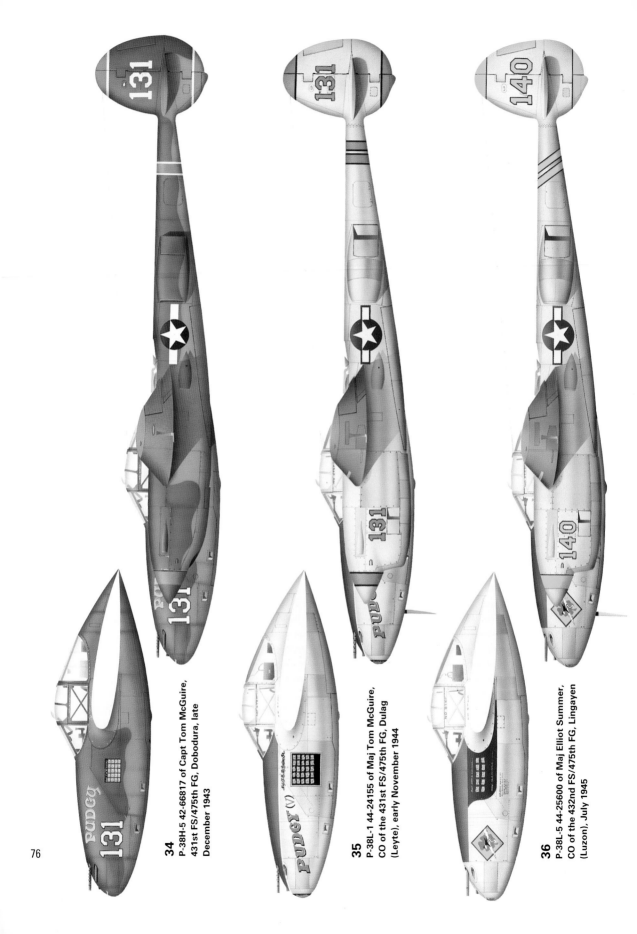

34
P-38H-5 42-66817 of Capt Tom McGuire,
431st FS/475th FG, Dobodura, late
December 1943

35
P-38L-1 44-24155 of Maj Tom McGuire,
CO of the 431st FS/475th FG, Dulag
(Leyte), early November 1944

36
P-38L-5 44-25600 of Maj Elliot Summer,
CO of the 432nd FS/475th FG, Lingayen
(Luzon), July 1945

58th FIGHTER GROUP

COL GWEN G ATKINSON
COMMANDING OFFICER
58th FG

From the actual experience of the past three years' active service, we know now that the glamorous times, so gaily phrased 'A feather in your cap and a motor in your lap', are gone, for fighters, especially in this theatre, have been required to assume a multitude of responsibilities.

Our operations boards, for example, during the past 15 months have carried eight different types of missions, in addition to the traditional alert and intercept activities. Fighter missions are now described as sweep, escort, strafe, glide-bomb, ship-bomb, reconnaissance, fire-bomb and close-support.

Fighter sweeps are designed to penetrate an area and clear it of all enemy aeroplanes. They are more or less cut and dried in planning and execution, since their variations are governed by the known factors of terrain, enemy anti-aircraft positions, targets, with their expected opposition, and the nature of our own 'strikes'. Included, of course, must be the freelancing target-of-opportunity type which raises merry Hell with the Japanese Air Force, not to mention its morale. Altitudes will vary from 5000-6000 ft for those looking for trouble, to 30,000 ft for those on the lookout for 'Sitting Ducks'.

The Japanese have suffered heavily from these freelance missions. Wewak proved to be a happy hunting ground, as did the Manila area during the Leyte, Mindoro and Luzon campaigns.

Escort missions are aimed at getting all aeroplanes being covered to the target and back by guarding them against successful attack. Close-support and top-cover comprise the elements of the mission, with altitudes varying, depending upon that of the escorted aeroplanes.

Strafing missions occupy a large percentage of our work, and include everything from harassing enemy troops, trucks, trains, barges, tanks, gun positions, tankers, oilers, troop and cargo ships, aeroplanes on the ground, equipment and supplies, to attacking destroyers, cruisers and battlewagons, both in the daytime and at night. Coupled with skip-bombing (to be discussed later), I believe that the largest percentage of our losses can be attributed to this type of mission.

There is no doubt in my mind that the toughest and roughest mission in which I have ever participated was a strafing mission which took place on the night of 26 December 1944. We were ordered to attack and disperse a Japanese naval task force, consisting of one heavy cruiser, one light cruiser and six destroyers, that was attacking Mindoro Island, in the Philippines. With nothing more than 50-calibre 'slugs' and 'guts', there having been insufficient time to bomb-up, we attacked with our P-47s.

If it were possible to fly through an open blast furnace I don't believe it would compare to the gunfire which opened up on us from those eight boats.

Twenty-nine from our group participated in the mission and how any of us came out alive is still a mystery to me. We did lose ten pilots and one badly injured, but five have since returned after baling out all over a 300-mile area. The Japanese force finally withdrew after a weak attempt at shelling the Mindoro strip, and did little damage. Information received since revealed that the reason lay in the fact that not only were two destroyers sunk on the spot, but also that practically all aiming devices, guns and crews of the remaining ships were damaged or knocked out. We did not claim that our P-47s inflicted all of the damage, for P-38s, P-40s and B-25s were also in on the deal, but we definitely feel that our eight 50 calibres contributed greatly to the successful repulsion of the attack.

The enemy in many ways is cagey. He places his anti-aircraft guns in some of the damndest places, moves them frequently, and has accounted for many of our losses in just this manner. In concentrated areas, their medium and light guns are wicked. However, we have experienced little difficulty with their heavy stuff. We have no trouble turning away from or under it.

We believe that surprise, speed, cover of approach, timing, concentration upon a single target and a slipping, skidding breakaway on the deck are the essential factors necessary for successful strafing. Spraying of a large area only wastes ammunition, and pulling-up after the attack is suicidal. The Japanese are always full of surprises. One neat trick they have pulled on us is to plant land mines, and when we come in on our strafing runs, set them off in our faces.

Glide-bombing first entered the picture when it was discovered that dive-bombing with the P-47 was not entirely satisfactory because of the speed picked up in the dive. In order to minimise our losses from ack-ack, we found it necessary to begin our dive not lower than 15,000 ft. We learned from practice that to achieve any degree of accuracy we had to use at least a 60-degree dive, and from that altitude and at that angle the P-47 picked up so much speed the pilot could not concentrate upon his diving for fear of an unsuccessful recovery.

We also learned that at speeds in excess of 325 to 350 mph, aileron buffeting was encountered when wing bombs (1000 lbs) or wing tanks (165 gallon) were carried. At present, we begin our glide, usually in two-ship elements, at 15,000 ft, hold our airspeed down to 325 mph, release our bombs between 7000 and 5000 ft, and either head for the deck or recover sharply up and to one side. Attacks are coordinated from different directions, and our bomb load varies from one 500-lb bomb under the belly to one 1000-lb bomb under each wing and a 500-lb bomb under the belly.

With practice, and practice alone, we have attained accuracy, for we have no sight designed for this bombing. The repeated practice of the same roll-in, turn and speed, the same angle of attack and the same method of releasing has improved our efficiency. To offset lag in releasing our bombs, we have wired our ships with electrical bomb releases.

Though the basic method of execution is the same, there are just as many variations of glide-bombing as there are pilots' bombing. I have found that by approaching the target from 90 degrees at 170 mph, placing the nose of the aeroplane on the target by executing a sharp pull-up wing-over turn, gradually reducing the angle of my dive as the speed increases and releasing the bombs at 6000 ft, I obtain my best results. Glide-bombing is only effective for area or strip coverage.

Light and medium bombers were doing it successfully, so when someone said 'Why not', we tried it, and another label was added – the P–47 skip-bomber. Since that time, dumping them out from masthead level and tree-top height has become standard operational procedure. With the sheet of lead thrown out by our eight 'fifties' preceding us to clear the way, we have been able on several occasions to utilise this method extremely effectively. Against shipping, it affords unlimited advantages, even to taking on the interference runners of the Japanese Navy.

When using a bomb load of only one 500 'pounder' slung under the belly, my approach is a shallow dive at about 370 mph, levelling off at around 50 ft and letting her go. From 1000 yards on in, I like plenty of lead coming from my guns, first to discourage, and, as I close, to reduce their return fire. With a much heavier bomb load – we carry up to

2500 lbs – I use the same procedure, but keep my speed down to 325 mph to avoid buffeting. Recently, one of our pilots dumped one 500 and two 1000 'pounders' right at the east entrance to the large tunnel on Corregidor. The great blast blew the doors to the tunnel open, and the next man in dumped a 1000 'pounder' slap-dab in the mouth of the tunnel. Using a four- to five-second delay fuse, little or no ill effect from the blast has been encountered.

On moonlight nights I believe gratifying results can be obtained, for I am certain that had we been lugging bombs the night of the 'Tokyo Express' to Mindoro, we could have sunk all of the destroyers and inflicted much crippling damage to the cruisers.

Keeping tab on the enemy in his movements is very difficult. He is more likely to pull the unpredictable than he is to follow a carefully laid out plan. Here again, the fighters have taken on added jobs. Reconnaissance is nothing more than covering an area with all eyes wide open, charting movements, shipping, locations of supplies, recording weather data, shadowing and picking up bits of information that will piece together the overall picture.

Fire-bombing, or the dropping of napalm bombs, which are ring tanks filled with a highly volatile mixture, is fairly new. Even so, in the short time we have been using them, devastating damage has been delivered. They have definitely proved, through tests and results, to be a very effective weapon. Good results have been obtained against pillboxes, gun positions, caves, buildings, troop concentrations and small boats. To me, this method of warfare is only in its infancy. There is no limit to its utilisation.

Close-support missions can certainly be said to cover a multitude of activities. Everything in the book can be used – from strafing to napalm bombing. On the majority of our missions over Luzon we were called upon at one time or another to support our ground forces. Beachhead cover flights are often required several times during one mission to clear out strong points in the enemy lines. These strong points may be dug-in fortifications, gun emplacements, pillboxes and sometimes even tanks. Close coordination and cooperation are necessary in order to eliminate the possibility of hitting our own forces.

There can be little doubt in anyones' mind that 'Fighters are here to stay'. As short-legged as our 'Jug' (P-47D-21) is, we are capable of carrying one 500-lb bomb a greater distance than our light bombers carry

Very few photographs of 58th FG P-47s have survived, this particular shot having been sourced from the logbook of a 311th FS pilot. Like all other Thunderbolt-equipped groups in the SWPA, the 58th initially marked its aircraft up with all-white tails and wing leading edges. Tasked primarily with flying ground attack sorties, the 58th FG scored just 14 confirmed kills during the Pacific War (*via John Stanaway*)

their load. We possess more strafing power, more speed and better manoeuvrability than the 'lights' and some of the 'mediums'. We have tangled with everything from row boats to heavy cruisers, training types to Zeros, wheel-barrows to tanks, 25 calibres to '105s, and we have come out on top.

This 311th FS/58th FG P-47D was photographed at Dobodura in early 1944. Its nickname appears to have only recently been applied, this machine having perhaps been passed onto the group by either the 35th or 348th FG upon the 58th's arrival in the SWPA in December 1943. *Billy Boy* was assigned to Lt W M Ritter (*via John Stanaway*)

MAJ EDWARD F RODDY
OPERATIONS OFFICER
58th FG

It has been several months since I have had contact with airborne enemy aircraft. However, I will endeavour to convey in this letter the tactics which I used then, and which I intend to use again soon. To make this letter as clear and concise as possible, and to keep from repeating myself, I will devote paragraph two to a few of the conceded practices upon entering into aerial combat.

A text could be written on the approach to combat, but the high spots are – to see the enemy first, then make sure that you aren't being baited, and decide upon a plan of attack and put it into action right away. After dropping wing tanks and advancing the throttle, all combat is commenced on a full tank of gas at a minimum indicated airspeed of 250 mph. My own personal point of view on how to fight the Japanese with minimum risk to my flight and myself, while administering maximum destruction to the enemy, is as follows.

DEFENSIVE TACTICS

When on the defensive, wingmen, flights, elements or however the case may be are well up in line abreast, with a little more than normal spacing laterally. Whether leading a squadron or smaller unit, there are only three situations which force me to take the defensive.

1. When the enemy fighters are above.

2. Men the enemy fighters are of superior numbers at level flight.

3. When the enemy fighters are firing before their presence is know.

Any situation other than those mentioned above, whether with fighters or bombers, puts me strictly on the offensive. Naturally, the prime objective when these situations arise is to reverse the set-up and get on the offensive as soon as possible. The methods for doing this are explained below.

When the enemy fighters are above, make them commit themselves before you expose the evasive tactics you are going to use. After the enemy

This photograph of Capt Ed Roddy was taken soon after he was made 'B' Flight leader of the 342nd FS/348th FG in November 1942. Note the squadron emblem painted beneath the cockpit of his P-47B. The 348th was destined to be the first Thunderbolt-equipped unit to see combat in the SWPA, although this machine was photographed whilst the group was based at Westover Field, Massachusetts (*via John Stanaway*)

Edward F Roddy

Edward Francis Roddy was born in Cleveland, Ohio, on 29 June 1919. He entered the Army Air Forces as an aviation cadet on 25 April 1941 and graduated with Class 41-1 at Foster Field, Texas, on 12 December that same year. After transitioning onto P-36 Hawk fighters, he was posted to the 56th Pursuit Group at Myrtle Beach, in South Carolina. Soon after Roddy had joined the group, it moved to Mitchel Field to provide air defence for New York. Here, he briefly flew the P-38 before the entire group transitioned onto the then new P-47B Thunderbolt.

On 30 September 1942, the 56th FG was split in half in order to form the 348th FG, which subsequently became the first Thunderbolt-equipped group to be sent to the SWPA. Roddy was amongst the cadre of pilots assigned to the new outfit, helping establish the 342nd FS. He was soon made the squadron's operation officer, and promoted

has committed himself, turn into him and, if possible, fire a head-on burst. After passing him, keep right on going, as this will put the greatest amount of distance between yourself and the enemy in the shortest period of time. Then work for altitude and prepare for offensive tactics,

When the enemy fighters are of superior number at level flight, the best defence is an aggressive offence. Make a head-on pass if possible, and go right through them, climbing at high speed as soon as you cease firing, striving again for altitude and a better set-up for going on the offensive.

When the enemy fighters are firing before their presence is known, immediate violent evasive action is called for, diving, if necessary, to get out of their range. Then strive to get the advantage on them by use of the tactics mentioned above.

OFFENSIVE TACTICS

Enemy bombers in this theatre are vulnerable to nose attack, being lightly armed forward compared to aft. So if the situation and time permit, these attacks should be favoured, and pressed home to point blank range. Aim for the leader and concentrate your fire on his most vulnerable parts – the engines and wing roots. Since the enemy bombers are going in the opposite direction, the heavy calibre tail guns will be in effective range for only a few seconds, and a violent turn in that period does not give them a chance to even swing their guns in the general direction of their attackers.

to captain on 26 January 1943. The group continued its lengthy work-ups at a series of east coast airfields until finally being posted to the Pacific in May 1943. Travelling by ship via Australia, the 348th eventually arrived in New Guinea in late July, and it was not until 5 November that Roddy got the chance to score his first kills – a Ki-61 and an A6M 'Hamp' shot down north-west of Wewak. He added further victories the following month, destroying two 'Zekes' on the 16th, a 'Dinah' on the 17th (giving him ace status) and two 'Bettys' on Boxing Day over Cape Gloucester. V Fighter Command claimed 62 victories on this day whilst defending the Allied Operation *Alamo* landings in the Arawe sector of New Britain. Roddy scored his final victory on 4 February 1944 when he downed a Ki-49 'Helen' bomber near Boram airfield.

One of the 348th FG's leading aces, Roddy was transferred to the recently-arrived 58th FG soon after scoring his last kill, joining the group as its operations officer. Promoted to major on 21 May, he served with the 58th FG until war's end, leading the group from 12 March 1945 until it returned to the United States. Remaining in the service post-war, Roddy flew both F-51s and B-26s in the Korean War, by which time he had attained the rank of full colonel. He later commanded the F-100 Super Sabre-equipped 48th Tactical Fighter Wing in England in the late 1950s, and also flew F-86D/Ls with the 112th Fighter Group, Pittsburgh Air National Guard, when it was assigned to Air Defense Command. Roddy retired from the USAF in February 1970, after which he attended the California State University and was employed there as safety director following the completion of his course. He retired from this position in 1987.

Since the enemy bomber formations are usually flat Vs, a stern approach should be started with a 2000- or 3000-ft shallow dive out of range to put yourself at the same altitude with a 100 mph advantage in speed. Then approach level, with about 30 to 40 degrees deflection, concentrating on the nearest aeroplane of the V, using him to block out the guns in the other ships of the formation. Stay on him until the deflection decreases to about ten degrees, breaking sharply away to the same side on which your pass originated. Coordinated attacks from any side are very effective in this case, as one aeroplane doesn't bear the brunt of the entire defensive fire.

The target afforded by an enemy fighter is very small, so the most effective passes are of 15 degrees or less deflection, from head-on or astern. Press these attacks home until you have to veer off to keep from ramming him. Do not reef the aeroplane into a turn or the indicated airspeed will drop off rapidly. Make your pass, fly out a short distance, turn around and come back for another pass. These deflections may seem to be very small, but I believe the majority of pilots, including myself, aren't expert deflection shots.

Capt Roddy poses with his P-47D-2 *Babs IV* (serial unknown) at Finschhafen soon after claiming his eighth, and last, kill on 4 February 1944. He was posted to the recently arrived 58th FG as group operations officer after allegedly clashing with senior officers within the 348th FG over the latter outfit's exclusive assignment of the more 'glamorous' strategic (bomber escort and fighter sweep) missions. This left the more mundane 'mud moving' sorties to be flown by the 58th FG (*via John Stanaway*)

Capt Roddy smiles for the camera in *Babs IV*, the fighter featuring kill decals for all eight of his victories (*via Anthony Kupferer*)

In my estimation, newly assigned pilots should concentrate on the following points:

1. Building up a technique for spotting 'Bogies'.

2. Fuel-saving tactics for long range missions.

3. Building up faith in instruments, especially compasses.

4. Homing procedures for lost aircraft.

5. Radio silence and air discipline.

6. Jungle kit essentials, and escape procedures.

LEADERSHIP AND CONTROL OF THE UNIT

Generally speaking, it is relatively easy to keep a squadron together if the mission is to patrol a convoy, escort bombers, or cover a landing. In these cases, the fighters have a central reference point, and usually stick pretty closely to the centre of activities. Against fighters, however, the squadron usually breaks down into the basic two-ship elements, and against Japanese bombers the four-ship flight remains intact. The radio is no longer a means of controlling the flight once the fight is started, and pre-arranged tactics and rendezvous points have to be utilised. The scarcity of enemy aeroplanes results in the over-eagerness of everyone on the flight, and there is often a mad scramble to see who will get to the enemy first, with all precaution thrown to the four winds. Were it not for the superiority of our equipment, our casualties would run much higher.

348th FIGHTER GROUP

Col Robert R Rowland
Commanding Officer
348th FG

This organisation was very fortunate when it arrived in this theatre in that we were able to live with and profit by the experience of other units which had been in combat for a year-and-a-half prior to our arrival. Those units, which were equipped with much more highly manoeuvrable fighters than our P-47s, had learned that even their ships were no match for the Zero in close-in fighting. Had we immediately been thrown into combat, our losses would probably have been high. However, we were given ample time to change our standard tactics as learned in our training in the States, and to fit them to this theatre.

Our original tactics were all concerned with extreme high altitude bomber escort and ground-controlled interception against an enemy equipped with aircraft having comparable service ceilings and armament, and using similar tactics.

We quickly found that the P-47 was untouchable as far as Japanese fighters were concerned in altitude performance, firepower, diving speed and ability to absorb enemy fire, but that slow speed climbs and close-in fighting made us easy prey to the enemy. During the months of August, September and October 1943, while 'breaking-in' slowly by escorting transports in comparatively safe areas, the combat tactics which later proved themselves over Wewak, Arawe, Cape Gloucester, Biak and later in the Philippines were evolved.

Lt Col Dick Rowland flew a succession of Thunderbolts nicknamed *Miss Mutt*, this particular machine being P-47D-4 42-22684. It was issued to the 348th FG CO as a replacement for battle-weary D-2 42-8096 in late November 1943, and is seen here at Finschhafen about a month later (*via John Stanaway*)

This photograph of P-47D-4 42-22684 was taken at Port Moresby in late November 1943, immediately after Dick Rowland's personal markings had been applied – including his tally of five victories. These were all scored in a P-47D-2, with the last two definitely being claimed in the original *MISS MUTT*. Eyewitness accounts from 348th FG personnel state that Rowland's final trio of victories were all scored in *MISS MUTT II*. Note the Fifth Air Force emblem painted onto the starboard wheel hub. A colour profile of this aircraft can be found on page 22 (*via John Stanaway*)

The thumb rule which advocates an aggressive, well timed, determined and coordinated attack as the best type of defence holds doubly true in the air, where you can't telegraph your punches and your opponent does not have a chance to get set. To have the attacker suddenly find himself being attacked was evidently not part of the Japanese training, because their formations quickly dispersed, and once they lost the initiative, they never seemed able to regain it.

If you are surprised from behind and above, the best defensive manoeuvre is a fast aileron roll down and to the right, coming out 180 degrees from your course at the time of the attack, and at an indicated air speed of at least 300 mph. This manoeuvre should not be executed too soon, but done just as the enemy is coming into firing range. The fast aileron roll of the P-47 will give him too much deflection for accurate shooting, and the ailerons on a Zero become so heavy at 300 mph that he will be unable to follow you in your diving turn and maintain the proper lead.

If you are attacked from above at low level, and the surprise is complete, the only defence is a flat skid. This manoeuvre is very deceptive, and affords a very difficult target. If, however, you discover the attack before the enemy is within range, your defence is to make a fast turn into him and go through shooting.

A good 'must' on defensive tactics is that of airspeed. Whenever a fight is certain, you should get rid of your external tanks and build up an indicated air speed of at least 250 mph by a slight dive, and never allow it to fall below that. At 250 mph, a P-47 in a high-speed climb will quickly out-distance any of the present Japanese fighters, and as was pointed out before, above 250-300 mph a P-47 possesses a much greater aileron rollability. Without this speed, it will be impossible for you to reverse that position and for you to assume the offensive.

The most important point is never to be jumped an the deck. Always maintain enough altitude so that if trouble develops you can use the superior diving power of the P-47 to its best advantage.

If the P-47's strong points are used to their best advantage, the offensive tactics are relatively easy in the SWPA. As no enemy fighter has an equal altitude performance, the most important point is to go over your target at extreme altitudes – 25,000 ft or higher. When patrolling at this altitude, you have plenty of time to stage your attack, taking advantage of weather, the sun, clouds, etc., so as to achieve complete surprise. The attack is made at very high speed, and if you are badly outnumbered and you continue right through the enemy formation, you can pull back up in a high-speed climb and be clear before a shot is fired at you. You can then continue toward home, or regain altitude into the sun and repeat the action. Four-ship flights of this unit have engaged Japanese fighter formations numbering 20 to 50, and consistently scored four to six victories in one pass without receiving a single bullet hole as long as the set rules were obeyed,

Never try to assume the offensive while below and under enemy fighters. Gain an equal or greater altitude by climbing out to one side and then coming back into them.

Another point is never to assume that you have achieved complete surprise until you see your strikes on the enemy aeroplane. The enemy will often maintain his formation until just prior to you opening fire, and then spring one of his trick manoeuvres, such as a 'Prince of Wales' – a very rapid turn into you – or one of his other tricks to catch the unwary. The only counter to such manoeuvres is to keep straight ahead, maintain your speed and try again. Any attempt to turn and fight him close-in is throwing away the best characteristics of your ship, and allowing him to use the superior qualities of his. Almost all of our air combat losses have been due to pilots becoming over-eager and forgetting this most important point.

Prior to our arrival in the Philippines, almost all of our strafing and skip-bombing missions were run against bypassed targets, where there was little or no chance of being jumped, and where almost all heavy and medium anti-aircraft weapons had been neutralised. Consequently, real

The groundcrew of Lt Col Rowland's original *Miss Mutt* (P-47D-2 42-8096) break from their work to pose for a group photograph at Port Moresby sometime after the fighter had been used to claim two 'Hamps' on 7 November 1943. Aside from the *Miss Mutt* titling, the Thunderbolt also featured female nose art and the inscription *PRIDE OF LODI OHIO* (Rowland's home town) just forward of the fuselage star and bar. Despite the aircraft's heavy useage and open air servicing in harsh tropical conditions, it was kept in immaculate condition, as this photograph clearly shows (*via John Stanaway*)

Robert R Rowland

Robert Richard 'Dick' Rowland was born in Lodi, Ohio, on 8 October 1917. He studied science at Ohio State and the University of Maryland, prior to joining the Army and commencing flight training on 25 January 1938. Rowland completed the pursuit course at Kelly Field, in Texas, on 1 February 1939, after which he served with the 1st Pursuit Group (PG) at Selfridge Field, Michigan, where he flew both the P-35 and the P-36. He was then sent to the Panama Canal Zone, where he again flew P-36s (and also the obsolete P-26 'Peashooter') with the 16th PG at Albrook Field. In December 1941, 1Lt Rowland returned to the United States to serve as Director of the Tuskegee Flying School in Alabama, overseeing the advanced fighter training of African American airmen.

Promoted to captain on 1 February and then major on 1 March 1942, Rowland secured

Lt Col Rowland receives the congratulations of Fifth Air Force CO Gen George Kenney in front of 348th FG at Finschhafen in early 1944. The group had performed remarkably well since first engaging the enemy in the SWPA on 16 August 1943, this success being primarily due to the effective leadership provided by original 348th CO Col Neel Kearby and his deputy Dick Rowland (*via John Stanaway*)

a posting back into the frontline in February 1943 when he joined the recently formed 348th FG as its executive officer at Providence, Rhode Island. He accompanied the unit to New Guinea several months later, and on 12 October 1943 he claimed his first kill when he destroyed a 'Dinah' over Wewak. Two further combats in November made him an ace, Rowland downing two Ki-61s on the 5th and two 'Hamps' on the 7th. By now a lieutenant colonel, Rowland was made CO of the 348th FG on 17 November after former boss Col Neel Kearby was posted to V Fighter Command. He claimed two more kills in December, destroying a 'Betty' bomber on the 26th and a 'Zeke' 24 hours later. Rowland scored his eighth, and final, victory on 27 February 1944 when he destroyed a 'Sally' bomber near Cape Hoskins airfield.

Rowland was made a full colonel on 15 May 1944, and he remained in charge of the group through to 8 June 1945, by which time it had exchanged its P-47Ds for P-51Ds. He stayed in the service post-war, becoming the first director of operations within the newly formed Strategic Air Command when it was activated in July 1946. A brief spell with the Central Intelligence Agency followed, after which Rowland was made CO of the F-86F-equipped 21st Fighter-Bomb Wing at George Air Force Base, in California. He also completed a tour with the military advisory group in Vietnam in 1964, and eventually retired from the USAF with the rank of major general in June 1968.

Col Dick Rowland prepares to depart on a mission from San Marcelino, on Luzon, in early 1945. He is sat in P-51D-15 44-15103, which was his final mount with the 348th FG. Rowland failed to score any kills flying the Mustang (*via William Hess*)

tactics, outside of mechanics, were never highly developed. However, during this operation we have been called on to attack well defended convoys, destroyers, operational airstrips and other targets of great value to the enemy. The following points are some of the principles concerning shipping strikes which we have learned.

Know your target's disposition, course and strength before take off. Plan your attack and have every man know his part of the plan. Approach your target high, and before you are in their sight circle around so that you come in out of the sun and/or using cloud cover. Before starting your attack, size up your target again to determine if your pre-flight intelligence was correct. The attack should be made on all targets simultaneously, and as a rule, three fighters should be allotted to each large transport and two to each destroyer. The actual attack should be made with ships line abreast in a fairly steep dive, levelling out at the point of bomb release and about masthead height. Strafing fire to neutralise ack-ack should be opened at about 800 yards' range, and continued all the way in. Air speed in excess of 400 mph is mandatory if losses are to be kept to a minimum.

The breakaway is accomplished by individual ships taking evasive action on the deck, and after they are clear of enemy fire, they reform and climb back to altitude. Should there be any chance of enemy interception, a normal patrol is kept at covering altitude to protect the strafer-bombers.

The tactics to be used in the strafing of enemy ground installations vary, of course, with the target and strength of the defence. Against undefended positions, a normal gunnery school pattern is used where individual gunnery is practiced. This also applies to low-level bombing. Against airfields, store areas and bridges, however, where strong defensive measures are to be expected, squadron and flight tactics must be used.

There are two methods of attacking strong installations. One is to come in high, make use of the sun and cloud cover, and depend primarily on speed to carry you through. The attack is made out of a steep curving dive, straightening out as you enter your strafing and/or bombing run. Every attempt is made to keep the flight in a line abreast formation, with individual ships firing on different targets. The breakaway is the same as on any other low level attack, making individual breaks, staying on the deck and reforming and climbing back up when out of ack-ack range.

If there is little or no return fire, the decision being the responsibility of the flight commander or squadron commander, as the case may be, more passes may be made and targets seen on the first pass destroyed. This, however, is a very dangerous practice, and against a reported well-defended target should never be attempted unless higher headquarters deems the losses worth the risk. Your surprise may have been complete on your first pass, and no defence was offered, but on your second pass they will be set and waiting.

The technique of flying over the target high, picking up a compass course out and then letting down to tree-top level when out of sight of the target, and turning to make a low altitude navigation run on the target, is not believed suitable for this theatre. The lack of towns, railroads, type of terrain and small size of our targets make this too much of a hit or miss proposition. It is also much more difficult for the individual pilots to do accurate gunnery, because on these approaches they have no opportunity to pick out and size up their targets until they 'pop

up' right at the edge of the field and start firing. The surprise that is achieved may be greater in this type of attack, but the lack of individual target assessment, difficulty of properly lining up on a target for a long accurate burst and the slow speed of breakaway, plus the chance of navigational errors, make it far less destructive and more difficult to execute than the high altitude, high-speed technique.

Also, if you are jumped in the comparatively slow run on the deck, you will be in serious trouble. In all these attacks, flights provide cover for each

Always one for unique personal markings on his various aircraft, Dick Rowland had P-51D-15 44-15103 adorned with a map of Ohio, complete with two stars – the top one was for his home town of Lodi, but the significance of the location of the second star remains a mystery (*via John Stanaway*)

Col Rowland also abandoned the *Miss Mutt* nickname when his group switched from Thunderbolts to Mustangs, christening his fighters *DIRTY DICK* instead. P-51D-15 44-15103 was the last machine to bear this sobriquet (*via John Stanaway*)

other, half of them attacking while the rest cover them at 6000 to 8000 ft. After delivering their attack, they climb back up and cover the others, who then go down and do their part.

It is not meant that any of these tactics are inflexible and absolute. They are all subject to change due to the status of training of the pilots, weather conditions, terrain, features, type of aircraft used, enemy defensive measures and innumerable other conditions. This letter was meant merely to transmit to you some of the basic principles, and the reasons for their adoption, with which this group has had some measure of success.

LT COL WILLIAM M BANKS
DEPUTY COMMANDER
348th FG

Looking back on 18 months of combat against the Japanese, we can readily realise how fortunate our group was to have had a well rounded and concentrated training programme before leaving the United States. However, most of that training had prepared us to meet an enemy with personnel and equipment comparable to our own, and for combat that would force our pilots to make maximum use of the high altitude characteristics of the Thunderbolt. Battle experience in the SWPA forced us to modify our tactics.

This was no insuperable problem, for each pilot had acquainted himself so thoroughly with the P-47 that after a short period marked by transport convoy and area patrols, plus constant advice from those who had fought the Japanese long prior to our arrival, he learned rapidly to favourably match the superior firepower, high altitude performance and diving speed of the P-47 against the manoeuvrability of the Japanese fighter. The consistent air discipline of our pilots also gave them an overwhelming advantage over the enemy, whose lack of organisation was obvious in so many instances.

During the days when the preponderance of Fifth Air Force operations were directed at Wewak, every effort was made to send frequent four-aeroplane fighter sweeps there to feel out the enemy, and to size up his aerial combat capabilities. From these Thunderbolt sweeps, we learned that the Japanese had a poor radar system, and that their air patrols were never above 26,000 ft and seldom above 15,000 ft. Many times we sighted enemy aeroplanes approaching their fields to land, and were able to dive to attack from above, shooting down the aeroplanes and climbing well out of range before their anti-aircraft gunners seemed fully aware of the situation.

When attacking enemy aeroplanes, we always tried to come in from astern and slightly above. If the enemy did see us, they would hold their formation until we came into range. Then a few of them would dive below, apparently to act as decoys, the others generally meeting our attack by executing a steep climbing turn into our attack, which forced us to shoot at maximum deflection. This technique on the part of the Japanese also put them in position to wing-over on the tail of any of our aeroplanes which might follow the enemy fighters whose initial reaction to our attack had been to dive to lower altitudes.

The Japanese loses all his manoeuvrability in a high speed dive, so he keeps his speed low by manoeuvring and gradually tries to work us down to the deck, thus causing us to lose the advantage of a quick diving breakaway. We quickly learned never to fall for a Japanese 'sitter', and never to turn more than 180 degrees with a Zero at any speed. Rather, we learned to fire at proper range, and to pull away in a high-speed climb not under 200 mph. Doing this, we could easily out-distance the enemy and get into position for further attacks.

We found it imperative for our security to stick to our two-aeroplane elements throughout combat. We also learned that it was wise to break off combat at around 6000 ft to make possible an easy breakaway. If our formations showed a tendency to become disorganised against superior numbers, we broke off combat at any altitude.

Throughout offensive operations, we always flew with a thorough knowledge of the outstanding advantages which our aeroplane had over the enemy. To make use of those advantages at every opportunity became second nature to us. They were;

1. High altitude performance.

2. Firepower.

3. High-speed diving ability.

4. The invulnerability of the P-47.

From our bomber escort missions we learned that the Japanese pilot, even when in a formation of superior numbers, will not attack our bombers, or our fighter escort generally, as long as our flights are well spaced and refuse to be sucked out of position. Often, Japanese pilots have made fake passes at our escort in order to break up the formation and create an opening to the bombers.

Maj Bill Banks named all of his fighters *Sunshine*, although the exact identity of this particular P-47D-23 remains unrecorded. Resting on its tail, and with a badly bent propeller, this machine appears to have suffered a forced landing. The photograph was taken at Tanuan, in the Philippines, in early 1945 (*via John Stanaway*)

William M Banks

William McGowan 'Bill' Banks was born in Raleigh, West Virginia, on 1 September 1915. He joined the Army Reserves and served as a flying cadet at Kelly Field, Texas, from 15 March through to 31 October 1941. Initially assigned to the P-40-equipped 62nd PS/ 56th PG, and flying in defence of New York following the Pearl Harbor attack, Banks transferred to the 90th FS/80th FG (again equipped with P-40s) at Bradley Field, Connecticut, in July 1942. Promoted to captain three months later, he was then sent literally across to the field to the newly-formed 342nd FS/348th FG and made CO on 2 November.

Equipped with the P-47 Thunderbolt, the group undertook lengthy work-ups at a series of east coast airfields before finally being posted to the Pacific in May 1943. Travelling by ship via Australia, the 348th arrived in New Guinea in late July and soon gave the Thunderbolt its combat debut in the SWPA. Flying P-47D-2 42-22532, which he nicknamed *SUNSHINE III*, Banks claimed his first kill (a Ki-43) on 13 September 1943. November saw him add a further three victories to his tally, with an 'Oscar' and a 'Zeke' destroyed over Wewak on the 15th and a Ki-46 downed in the same area on the 25th. Banks 'made ace' with a second 'Dinah' victory on the morning of 20 December. He was promoted to major on 31 January 1944, and exactly one week later Banks destroyed a Ki-61 east of Cape Gloucester for his final kill of his first tour. Returning home on 24 May, he rejoined the group several months later as a staff pilot with the 348th FG HQ.

Flying in support of the invasion of the Philippines, the group moved to the recently liberated island of Leyte in early November, where it took up residence at Tacloban Field. From here its pilots would fly long-range bomber escort missions in their P-47D-23s, accompanying B-24s as they hit Japanese airfields and industrial targets. A great number of these missions, as well as fighter sweeps, were flown in December, and 'Bill' Banks scored his final kills during the course of the month. On the 11th he destroyed a 'Zeke 32', and on Christmas Eve, during a raid on Clark Field, in the Philippines, he destroyed two more 'Zekes' over Floridablanca airfield.

Banks was made a lieutenant colonel on 2 February 1945, and later that month the 348th transitioned from the P-47D to the P-51D/K Mustang at San Marcelino, on Luzon. He was made group CO on 8 June, and remained in command until 26 November, by which time the unit was based at Ie Shima, in Japan. Banks served in the Army Air Force post-war until finally retiring in June 1963. He passed away on 6 May 1983 in San Antonio, Texas.

Maj Banks looks every inch the SWPA fighter pilot in this photograph, taken at Tanuan, on Leyte, in December 1944. He would score his final three kills during the course of this month, taking his overall tally to nine victories. This is almost certainly the aircraft seen on page 93 (*via John Stanaway*)

In a number of instances, our bomber formations had to be escorted by approximately half of the original escort because of the snafus en route to the target. This situation placed the remaining escort in a doubly responsible position, and generally afforded the enemy greater opportunity for successful attack. In such situations our flights would do some faking of their own, firing scare bursts simultaneously, but never losing their positions over the bombers. The Japanese have always respected our firepower, and generally in such cases as these they would break off their attacks without inflicting damage.

It must be remembered that fighter escort must stay with the bombers regardless of loss. Well coordinated close, medium and top cover is the best protection we can offer bombers and our own escorting fighters.

Several times on fighter sweeps our fighters have been surprised by enemy patrols, sometimes of superior strength. Our best reaction to surprise attack was an uncoordinated roll, a diving get away and a 180-degree change of direction. The Japanese would seldom follow a high-speed dive because they lose their own manoeuvrability at 300 mph or over. This manoeuvre on our part placed us in a position for a high-speed climb back to an altitude of advantage.

On dive-bombing attacks, we have found that by releasing our bombs from wing shackles our accuracy has been increased 75 per cent over the results of the old glide-bombing technique. Full advantage should be taken of the position of the sun and clouds when dive-bombing to create surprise and provide for a good breakaway.

NEVER attempt to turn more than 180 degrees with a Zero.

NEVER attempt to fight with your wing tanks attached.

NEVER fail to stick to the two-aeroplane element throughout combat.

NEVER allow less than 6000 ft to break away in case of trouble.

A skip-bombing target must be studied whenever possible before the mission, especially if the attack is to be made against shipping or other targets that may offer heavy ack-ack. Points to be considered are – number, type and position of enemy vessels, weather over the target, position of the sun at time-on-target, possible enemy air opposition and expected enemy fields of fire.

When the target is sighted, each flight should pick a definite objective. Troop transports can be easily knocked out by two P-47s making a well timed attack. Destroyers should be attacked by at least four aeroplanes. Flights should approach their targets in a fairly steep dive, flying line abreast. All aeroplanes should begin to strafe a little beyond range in order to neutralise or confuse enemy anti-aircraft fire. The bombs should be released at a very low altitude and at the pull up point of the dive. Once you commit yourself, press the attack and leave the area at as fast a speed as you can.

Most of the strafing targets that have been assigned to our group have been pretty well worked over by heavy and medium bombers before we have reached them, so that most of the heavy and medium ack-ack has been knocked out. However, our aeroplanes have constantly been subjected to light machine gun fire. The anti-aircraft dispersal by the Japanese at many of our targets has been questionable, so we have found that playing safe when in doubt pays dividends. Weather, cloud cover and terrain features naturally afford many opportunities for increasing the

P-51K-10 44-12073 *SUNSHINE VII* was flown by 348th FG Col Bill Banks from Ie Shima during the final months of the war in the Pacific. Colourful stripes on the spinner and through the fighter's nickname denoted the four squadrons within the group (the 348th FG was the only group in V Fighter Command to control four units). The three Mustangs behind the lead fighter belonged to the 341st FS (*via John Stanaway*)

efficiency and safety with which strafing attacks and breakaways can be performed.

When undefended targets are hit, a normal ground gunnery pattern may be used with great effect. But it is desirable to approach heavily defended targets from the direction of the sun, through the clouds, or with maximum use of all favourable terrain features. Flights go in in four-aeroplane formations, generally line abreast. Two-aeroplane attacks are also effective. We have tried never to return for another pass at the same target from the same direction on the same day.

It is to be realised that the comments and suggestions appearing in this letter are not offered as hard and fast rules of conduct. They do grow, however, from the opinions of the writer, and of those men with whom he has flown, who have formed them after 18 months of Thunderbolt flying against the enemy in the SWPA. All factors being fairly normal, the techniques described herein have proved themselves to be, through experience, most effective.

CAPT MARVIN E GRANT
342nd FS/348th FG

Every fighter pilot has undoubtedly read reams of material on combat and advanced theories of all the technical data, and still wonders what he himself would do under combat.

In defensive combat, unless completely surprised, the superior speed the P-47 has over the enemy can turn the defensive position into an offensive one in a matter of seconds. At altitude, a sharp turn downward to the right will break up an enemy pair, and then a high-speed climb to gain back the altitude lost will put you in a position to attack. You practically have to have your head up all the way to be shot down from the rear by a Japanese pilot. At minimum altitude, violent cross-controlling will act as a safeguard.

If the enemy has a definite altitude advantage over you, and attacks anywhere from 'four o'clock' to 'nine o'clock', a sharp chandelle into him will give you a chance for a deflection shot, as the Japanese pilot will break away. The only type of enemy fighter that has traded a head-on pass with me has been a 'Tony'. With the superior amount of firepower the P-47 has over its opponent, you can fire out of range and the enemy will break.

In the offensive (individually), the wingman must fly close enough to take advantage of any error that the leader may make. All the basic instructions are the best suited, but to take advantage of that split-second opportunity, one must know exactly what he is going to do.

Anyone can shoot down the enemy if he is sitting on his tail, but to get onto his tail first is what counts. Haphazard approaches and firing out of range have lost many a victory for the over-eager fighter pilot.

In the leadership and control of the unit, not enough emphasis can be placed on the absolute control and confidence the leader must have from his men. Minimum excitement can be expected from a flight if the leader shows calmness and coolness before and during an attack. If going on a long mission, it is very essential that a well-guarded flight must be kept, and yet the flight should be loose enough to permit the least amount of fatigue. The flight should be well up, and stepped up, to cover each other and the elements at all times within a radius that allows turning distance into an attack from behind. Flying the element too close to the leader tends to load too much responsibility onto the flight leader.

In the defence of the flight being attacked, the enemy will seldom strike a well balanced flight, and on the occasions that they have, the fight

Capt Marvin Grant's P-47D-23 42-27886 sits in the 342nd FS dispersal area on Leyte in late 1944, the aircraft carrying a single 500-lb bomb on its centreline rack and tanks attached to its wing pylons. Although the seven-kill ace failed to claim any victories with this machine, he used the immaculate Thunderbolt to attack Japanese troops on a near-daily basis during the campaign to retake the Philippines (*via William Hess*)

Marvin E Grant

Marvin Eugene Grant was born in Racine, Wisconsin, on 21 October 1916. A sixth cousin of Ulysses S Grant, the legendary Union general in the American Civil War, Marvin Grant developed a keen interest in aviation at an early age. As a teenager he worked as an apprentice mechanic on a World War 1-era de Havilland DH 4, and eventually flew solo on this machine. Grant attended the University of Wisconsin upon his graduation from high school and then joined the Army Reserves. Accepted as an aviation cadet in December 1941, he graduated with Class 42-1 at Moore Field, Texas, on 9 October 1942. Grant was then posted to the newly formed 342nd FS/348th FG at Bradley Field, Connecticut, the unit taking delivery of its first aircraft (P-47Bs) just days later. The 342nd was the first unit assigned to the group, and it took some time for the squadron to receive its full allocation of aircraft.

The 348th spent eight months working up to combat status, and in May 1943 it left for the Pacific aboard the Army transport vessel *Henry Gibbons*. After a long and arduous trip, the unit eventually arrived in New Guinea, after acclimatising in Australia, in late June. Flying from Port Moresby, Marvin Grant finally registered his first kill on 16 December when he downed a B5N 'Kate' torpedo-bomber north of Arawe whilst supporting the Allied landings on New Britain. Ten days later he destroyed a G3M 'Betty' bomber near Umboi Island.

More action came the 348th FG's way when the group covered the Allied landings on Arawe and Biak islands, Grant claiming a 'Tony' destroyed over the latter location on 27 May. Eight days later he became an ace when he destroyed two 'Zekes' 40 miles east of Biak, and then scored his final victories (two 'Kates') on 12 June in roughly the same location. Promoted to captain soon afterwards, Grant became the squadron's operations officer in October 1944 and eventually completed his tour with the unit in the Philippines in February 1945. He had flown 187 combat missions.

Grant remained in the USAF until 31 March 1962, by which time he had risen to the rank of lieutenant colonel. Entering the teaching profession once back in civilian life, he served as a school administrator for 15 years in Denver, Colorado, before retiring for a second time in 1977.

1Lt Marvin Grant poses with his P-47D-4 42-22694 *Racine Belle* at Finschhafen in December 1944. Aerial success eluded the future ace in this particular machine (*via William Hess*)

was soon changed into the offensive by having a well balanced and controlled flight.

In the offensive, it is hard to maintain flights together, although elements work well together, and depending upon the type of formation you are attacking, two-ships will have the best of success in all dogfights. It is essential that radio contact be kept at all times.

When attacking Japanese aeroplanes from the rear, and I am certain that they have seen me, I usually fire a short burst out of range to make them commit themselves. Their manoeuvrability makes it impossible to get in a good deflection shot at close range. By firing a burst out of range, and making the enemy commit himself, one can still get the proper lead by the time he is in range. This has proved successful on two different occasions.

MAJ WILLIAM D DUNHAM
460th FS/348th FG

I feel it a privilege to write to you about my experience in fighter tactics in the Southwest Pacific, and I hope that my comments, along with those of other pilots who have had similar experience in this theatre, will prove helpful in better preparing new Thunderbolt pilots for their part in our work.

In this theatre, the best individual defensive tactic is a hard and fast offensive, regardless of the odds. This tactic, used in defence, takes full advantage of the superior speed and diving ability of the P-47. It permits a pass at the enemy and a fast dive away with little danger of being shot down.

If you are attacked from above while you are at cruising speed, and the attacking aeroplanes have excessive speed, the best defensive manoeuvre is a sharp aileron roll to the right and down, diving out 180 degrees from the direction of the attack. This manoeuvre cannot be started too soon, but must be executed just before the attacking aeroplane is within range. The slow aileron action of the Japanese fighters at high speeds makes it impossible for them to pull through far enough to get the proper lead, and by the time he can change direction you should have enough speed to easily outdistance him.

If attacked from above when you are on the deck, and you do not see the enemy soon enough to turn into him for a head-on pass, the best immediate defensive manoeuvre is a gentle skid. The average Japanese pilot will not correct for skid unless it is very noticeable. In one case, a 'Tony' pilot expended all his ammunition without a single hit while firing from dead astern position at a range of 100 yards.

There are two basic principles for defensive tactics. These are altitude and speed. Airspeed of 250 mph must be maintained and a sufficient altitude should be kept to permit full use of the P-47's diving speed. This can be considered to be 5000 ft as a minimum.

In offensive individual combat there are two principles to observe. First, never attack unless you have an equal or greater altitude than the enemy. Secondly, plan your attack to afford the greatest element of surprise. An altitude advantage of at least 10,000 ft does not guarantee surprise, but it does offer the greatest odds in favour of securing this advantage. While fly-

ing four-ship fighter sweeps with Col Kearby, we made it a policy to go in at 26,000 ft or above. At this altitude, they could neither see or hear us on the ground, while it was easy for us to see the enemy landing or taking off. Our attack was invariably from the stern, with the sun to our advantage. In every case we were firing before the enemy knew we were around.

Excessive speed of the P-47 in such a diving attack permits a rapid recovery of the altitude advantage begun with. At a speed of 350 mph or more, one can easily pull up and hammerhead back down into the fight. In such an attack, and in all attacks on the enemy, it is imperative that no turn greater than 90 degrees be attempted before breaking off the attack.

When attacked from the rear or side, the Japanese pilot will frequently hold his course until you are in firing range, and then turn sharply, making it impossible for you to get a proper lead. A good way to counteract this defence manoeuvre is to open up at 500 or 600 yards in order to induce him to make this manoeuvre in time for you to get sufficient lead. Ninety per cent of the time, the enemy pilot will start his turn at the first sight of tracers, thus giving you time for sufficient leading. In one case my opponent turned so sharply that I finished the pass head-on.

With the additional power afforded by water injection, one can attack from an equal altitude and climb army in a high-speed climb until sufficient distance is acquired to make a head-on pass.

One of the main factors in effective leadership and control of the unit in the air is proper briefing. Briefing cannot be successful unless only one construction can be taken from the information presented. The action contemplated must be uniformly interpreted by each member of the mission. Instructions cannot be so ironclad as to prevent flexibility to meet unexpected situations. But there must be no doubt concerning the course to be flown to and from the target, nor any lessening of a healthy respect for weather. It is common knowledge that weather is the biggest, most inflexible enemy in this theatre.

Leadership, of course, cannot be obtained by talk, or maintained by sporadic practice. It can only be accomplished by constant emphasis throughout the training programme, and afterwards, a continuance with no opportunity given for slackening. All training must be aimed at the most strict air discipline. This alone, however, is not enough. It can only be considered supplemental to daily corrective action against the smallest deviation from complete air discipline. Such action should be immediate.

Above
Undoubtedly the 348th FG's most colourful Thunderbolt, P-47D-23 42-27884 *Bonnie* was the mount of 460th FS CO Maj Bill Dunham for much of the group's campaign in the Philippines. And it was definitely more than just a 'show pony', for Dunham used it to claim five kills in two missions on 7 and 14 December 1944, thus taking his tally to 15 victories (as shown beneath the cockpit) (*via John Stanaway*)

Above Right
P-51K-10 44-12017 *"MRS. BONNIE"* was the final wartime fighter assigned to Bill Dunham in the Pacific, the aircraft being issued to him at around the same time as he was promoted to lieutenant colonel and made deputy CO of the 348th FG. Dunham used it to claim his last kill, on 1 August 1945, and the Mustang is seen here at Ie Shima soon after being adorned with a 16th victory symbol to mark this event. This aircraft is featured in colour profile on page 74 (*via John Stanaway*)

Below
A group of 342nd FS/348th FG pilots assemble around Lt Col Dunham's P-51K for a VJ-Day photograph at Ie Shima in September 1945. A 342nd FS Mustang is parked behind the Dunham machine
(*via John Stanaway*)

If it cannot be accomplished during the flight, it must be taken up as soon after landing as possible.

One of the most common failings among new pilots is carelessness in formations, in landing patterns and in taxiing. They must be checked promptly. Moreover, among new pilots I've noticed a decided absence of appreciation for the need to conserve gas, or if appreciated, an ignorance of how the saving of gas can be best accomplished. A wingman who plays

the turns 'smart' can come home with more gas than his leader. It is a worthwhile objective for a new pilot.

Squadron defensive tactics vary greatly according to the type of mission, and the position of the squadron on the mission. On a patrol or an area cover mission, it is necessary that the flights in the squadron are in close support of each other, and that the leader has complete control. On this type of mission, as in individual combat tactics, the best defence is a fast offence, with the same advantage factors of altitude, surprise and sun being of vital importance. Once the enemy is contacted, it is almost always necessary to split the squadron in order to use squadron firepower to its greatest advantage. Such a division must be an orderly one, not losing by it the coordinated action of flight or element, nor can it be permitted to

William D Dunham

William Douglas 'Dinghy' Dunham was born on 29 January 1920 in Tacoma, Washington. Growing up in Nezpeace, Idaho, he attended the University of Idaho from 1937 to 1940, before joining the Army Reserves and serving as a flying cadet at Luke Field, Arizona, from 26 April through to 11 December 1941. He was then posted to the Panama Canal Zone, where he spent nine months flying P-39s with the 53rd PG from Howard Field. Dunham was then transferred back to the USA in November 1942 to join the newly formed 342nd FS/348th FG, which had just been equipped with P-47 Thunderbolts.

Following many months working up, the group finally made it to the Pacific in late June 1943, by which time Dunham had been promoted to captain. He claimed his first kill – a 'Tony' – on 11 October east of Boram, and followed this up with two 'Haps' south of Malang five days later. His final score in October came on the 19th when he engaged a relatively rare F1M 'Pete' observation seaplane east of Wewak, which he swiftly shot down. Dunham had to wait until 21 December to add to his score, and he made the most of his opportunity by destroying three 'Val' dive-bombers in quick succession while on patrol over the Japanese stronghold of Arawe. Having achieved 'ace-dom', Dunham then returned home on 90 days' leave.

He commenced his second tour in early March 1944, and claimed his eighth and ninth kills on the 5th of that month when he destroyed a G3M 'Nell' bomber and an 'Oscar' over Wewak. Dunham was given command of

Bill Dunham clearly had an active war, claiming 16 kills (the final one was downed some months after this shot was taken), sinking two Japanese vessels and undertaking some 30 bombing missions. This was the scoreboard that adorned his P-47D-23 42-27884, which appears in colour profile on page 74 (*via John Stanaway*)

degenerate into a number of individual, uncoordinated actions. Element and flight members must stay with their leaders, and in any event the most important axiom of all is to at least keep in pairs.

On escort missions, especially when flying close cover, it is necessary to have your flights in position to cover another flight if it is attacked. This is accomplished by carrying your flights in a staggered line abreast, with enough space between flights to work scissors or the 'break and slide in behind' principle. The enemy will almost invariably attack the fighter cover first to disrupt it, before going after the bombers. When a squadron of fighters is covering a section of bombers, the support of flights is best accomplished by having ships on either side – about 1000 ft above and 500 to 1000 ft to either side of the bomber formation. The medium cover

the 342nd FS when Maj Bill Banks returned home on leave in late May, and two months later he was made CO of the newly established 460th FS, which became the 348th FG's fourth squadron. Promoted to major on 20 September, Dunham broke his scoring drought on 18 November when he shot down a 'Zeke' off Camotes Island.

By now the group was conducting long-range fighter sweeps and escort missions over the Philippines in preparation for the coming invasion, and on 7 December Dunham enjoyed his best day in the SWPA. Supporting the allied landings at Ormoc Bay, V Fighter Command's P-38s and P-47s accounted for over 50 aircraft shot down. Fifteen of these were claimed by 348th FG pilots, with no fewer than 14 being credited to the 460th FS. The squadron's leading pilot on the day was none other than the CO, 'Dinghy' Dunham, who destroyed two 'Zeke 32s' and two Ki-43s. Seven days later he added a Ki-21 'Sally' to his growing tally, forcing the bomber down into the sea off Talisay during an early-morning sweep.

On 18 December Dunham was transferred to the 348th FG HQ as its assistant operations officer, before briefly returning home in early 1945 to attend a gunnery school set up for future Mustang pilots. He rejoined the 348th FG as its operations officer in May, by which time the group had traded in its P-47D-23s for P-51D/Ks, and embarked on a series of base moves that eventually saw it end up at Ie Shima, on Okinawa, on 9 July. Later that month Dunham was promoted to lieutenant colonel and made deputy group CO, and he celebrated by downing a Ki-84 'Frank' over Kyushu during a long-range fighter sweep of the Japanese home islands on 1 August 1945.

Having finished the war with 16 confirmed kills, Dunham chose to remain in the Army Air Force. He briefly served as CO of the F-84E Thunderjet-equipped 31st Fighter Escort Wing, based at Turner Air Force Base in Georgia, in mid 1951, and then headed the F-84F Thunderstreak-equipped 12th Fighter-Day Wing at Bergstrom Air Force Base, Texas, from August 1956 through to its deactivation in January 1958. Promoted to brigadier general on 1 August 1963, Dunham was the Seventh Air Force's deputy chief of staff for operations during the early stages of the Vietnam War before retiring from the USAF in June 1970. He succumbed to lung cancer in Issaquah, Washington, on 3 March 1990.

Aside from the addition of a 16th rising sun, the tally board applied to Lt Col Dunham's P-51K looked little different to the one worn on his P-47D-23 in late 1944 (*via John Stanaway*)

must stay in the same area as the bomber formation to give support to close cover and break up attacking aircraft. The top cover is never on the defensive, and should attack the enemy well ahead of the bomber formation. If this is accomplished, the Japanese will always 'run into the house' without attempting to attack the bombers.

MAJ WALTER G BENZ JR 342nd FS/348th FG

The following ideas and suggestions are the results of problems and experience gained by our pilots while flying the P-47 Thunderbolt.

As individuals, and as a working team, our best defensive is definitely a good aggressive offensive. If attacked at an altitude above 10,000 ft, we have always been able to dive away from the enemy. The dive may be made either as a shallow or steep dive. The steep dive is used when the enemy is directly on your tail. At any altitude, we have been able to out-run their aeroplanes, but it is important not to let your airspeed get low for the enemy has a much greater acceleration at low speeds than we do. We have used a high-speed climb to great advantage. In some instances, the climb can be made directly into the sun, and make a wing-over. The enemy is unable to see the manoeuvre, which will probably put us in an offensive position. In the event that we are caught on the deck, we skid and fly uncoordinated, and make use of any scud or low cloud cover.

When we attack a fighter, we go in at high speed, and as a breakaway we use a high-speed climb. If the fighter should see you approaching him and he starts to turn, follow only long enough to get lead and open fire if it is possible for you to get enough lead. Do not turn with them under any circumstance. Climb back up and come in for another pass. If the enemy should do a half roll and dive, follow him and you can usually get him. The best attack under favourable conditions is at high speed dead astern and just a little below the enemy fighter, then run up his tail before opening fire to assure surprise.

The squadron formation we use the most is four flights of four in extended two-ship elements. The elements are well up to form a slightly staggered line abreast, and the flights are also well up almost in line abreast. The second section is 500 to 1000 ft above the first section. This enables the squadron leader to see all his flights, and also gives him good control of the unit.

The importance of staying together cannot be over-emphasised. Never be left alone, and never leave a man to himself. If you are broken up in a fight, always remain in pairs – wingmen must stay with their leaders. If you find yourself alone, do all you can to join with a flight or some other friendly aeroplane.

Bomber cover varies greatly with the type of mission and the amount of fighter cover assigned. When we are close cover to a high altitude bombing mission, we usually keep our flights about 1000 ft above, with one section on each side of the bomber formation, and the lead flights are slightly ahead of the bombers.

When we are covering low altitude bombers and strafers, we usually have a top cover of fighters, and in addition provide close cover with two flights, about 500 ft away, on each side of the bombers. As we approach the target, we pull up to about 2000 ft, then increase throttle and go in at high speed so we can meet any enemy attack with minimum disadvantage. On a cover of this type, we were usually unable to turn into the enemy, but let them fly through us and then we hit them as they attacked the bombers. This was made possible because of our going in at very high speed, and flying so that we had mutual protection.

We have been lucky in that we have very seldom been on the defensive for very long. In one fight, we had a four-ship formation hit by eight enemy fighters with a 15,000-ft advantage. We shot down four with no losses because we saw them coming and, most importantly, stayed in two-ship elements.

Future 342nd FS CO Jim Benz flew a series of Thunderbolts and Mustangs christened *Dirty Old Man* during his three-and-a-half years with the 348th FG. This P-47D-2 (serial unknown) was the most successful of his many mounts, for he used it to claim four kills and one probable between 22 September and 26 December 1943. Seen here at Finschhafen in early 1944, the fighter's olive drab cowling was fitted to a replacement natural metal Thunderbolt several months after this photograph was taken (*via John Stanaway*)

Walter G Benz Jr

Walter Gottlieb 'Jim' Benz Jr was born on 27 December 1919 in St Louis, Missouri. He joined the Army Reserves on 26 September 1941 and graduated from pilot training on 29 April 1942 at Ellington Field, in Texas. Following his transition onto the

Thunderbolt, Benz transferred to the 342nd FS/348th FG soon after the group's formation on 30 September 1942. He accompanied the 348th to the SWPA, arriving in Port Moresby, New Guinea, in late June 1943.

Thrown into action within days of his arrival, Benz scored his first victory on 22 September (two weeks after being promoted to captain) when he destroyed a lone K-46 'Dinah' conducting a late-morning reconnaissance of Finschhafen. His next two kills came during escort missions for

Capt Benz gets to grips with his paperwork in the 342nd FS Operations tent at Finschhafen in early 1944. Possibly the 348th FG's longest serving pilot, he would eventually become its last CO. Benz led the group from November 1945 through to its disbandment in May 1946 (*via John Stanaway*)

B-24 and B-25 bombers, Benz claiming a 'Tony' on 22 October and a 'Hamp' (also listed as an 'Oscar') on 15 November.

He scored his fourth victory whilst the 348th FG was supporting the Operation *Alamo* landings at Cape Gloucester, in New Britain, on 26 December. More than 100 V Fighter Command aircraft were given the job of protecting the Allied convoy moored off the beachhead, and they were kept busy repelling persistent Japanese aerial attacks. Some 62 claims were lodged by US airmen on this day, 17 by pilots from the 348th FG. One of these was a G4M 'Betty' bomber downed by Benz east of Sakar Island at 1700 hrs.

Made CO of the 342nd FG on 26 July 1944 and promoted to major on 7 October, 'Jim' Benz had to wait almost a full year before he could claim his all-important fifth kill. By then the group had moved to Leyte, in the Philippines, and was conducting fighter sweeps across the region in support of the allied push northwards. It was during one such mission to Cebu on 11 December that Benz destroyed a Ki-43 to take his tally to five kills, thus making him an ace. Four days later he downed a 'Zeke 52' over Semirara Island, then claimed two more on the 20th when he led his unit on a strafing attack on Mindoro airfield. Remaining with the group after it had swapped its Thunderbolts for Mustangs and then moved closer to Japan, Benz actually led the 348th FG from 26 November 1945 through to its deactivation in May 1946.

He remained in the Army Air Force post-war, seeing further combat with the 8th Fighter-Bomb Group during the Korean conflict – here, he flew the F-80 Shooting Star and then the F-86 Sabre. 'Jim' Benz retired from the USAF with the rank of colonel in 1970.

Maj Benz's final four kills were all claimed in this machine, P-47D-23 *DIRTY OLD MAN 4th* (serial unknown). These were scored between 11 and 20 December 1944 while he was leading the 342nd FS from Tacloban (*William Hess*)

We generally keep our external tanks until the enemy has been sighted, and have always had time to turn into the attack, or to dive away and then use a high-speed climb to get on even terms and come back into the fight.

If we spot the enemy below us, we have found that by sending down one flight of four at a time, the first flight will hit and break up the formation. Then the next flight goes down to help anyone who has picked up a fighter on his tail, and also to catch any stragglers. Each successive flight has the same job – to help anyone in trouble, and to get the stragglers as the Japanese flights are broken up more with each successive flight in which our pilots attack. The number of enemy aeroplanes to be attacked has had little effect on us, for with an altitude advantage, or on even terms, we will attack at odds of ten-to-one. This has been done with success.

Our operations in this theatre have been long range since our arrival in the SWPA. Most of our targets are from 350 to 500 miles away, and in some instances over that distance. This has meant special training of new pilots in the operation of the P-47 in order to obtain minimum fuel consumption. The sweating out of gas over long stretches of jungle or hundreds of miles of open sea is definitely fatiguing to the pilot. The importance for pilots to know their aeroplane, and to fly it to maximum performance, cannot be over-emphasised. It is very important that pilots be aggressive, and have a keen desire to fight. A competitive spirit between flights helps to develop this attribute in the squadron.

475th FIGHTER GROUP

COL CHARLES H MACDONALD
COMMANDING OFFICER
475th FG

The formation we fly is what we call out here the standard US formation. It is a four-ship flight, with the elements staggered and flexible. It is simple and easy to fly, yet the leader has visual and positive control. The disposition of the squadrons depends on the type of mission.

When one gets over the target, the flights fall into the fighting formation. That is, each flight forms itself into a loose string. These strings are mutually supporting, and when they are weaving and criss-crossing, present an extremely difficult nut to crack.

That, in brief, is our disposition going out and over the target. In the fight, we stress the importance of keeping the flight intact. The wingmen should never lose the element leader.

The main reason we beat the enemy is because we work as a team, using the good qualities of our aeroplanes and keeping him from using the good qualities of his own. I think if the Japanese had P-38s and we had Zeros, we could still beat them because the average American pilot is a good team worker and is always aggressive.

If I were to pick out the most valuable personal traits of a fighter pilot, aggressiveness would rate high on the list. Time and again, I have seen quick aggressive action, even from a disadvantageous position, completely

The wreckage of 433rd FS P-38H-1 'white 193', which Maj MacDonald hastily commandeered in order to engage 'Val' dive-bombers as they passed overhead the 475th FG's Dobodura base on 15 October 1943. The future 27-kill ace claimed his first two victories (and two damaged) during this mission, cutting a swathe through the ranks of the Rabaul-based 582nd *Kokutai*. MacDonald spotted the 'Vals' just as the wheels of his fighter left the ground, and he proceeded to maul a formation of seven dive-bombers as they retreated back to their New Britain base. Protecting the 'Vals' were no fewer than 39 Zeros from the 204th *Kokutai*, and one of these set upon the lone Lightning – MacDonald had become separated from his wingman soon after take off. The P-38's left engine and electrical and hydraulic systems were shot out and fuel tanks punctured, although MacDonald managed to limp back to Dobodura (*via John Stanaway*)

Each of 'Mac' MacDonald's assigned Lightnings were named *PUTT PUTT MARU*, with this particular example being P-38L-1 44-24843. It was almost certainly used by the 475th FG CO to claim 13 kills between 10 November 1944 and 1 January 1945, thus making it one of the USAAF's most successful Lightnings in terms of aerial victories. This aircraft was lost on 2 January 1945 whilst being flown by 432nd FS CO, and five-kill ace, Capt Henry Condon. The latter was leading a bomber escort mission to airfields in the Manila area when he spotted a troop train. Leading his pilots in on a strafing pass, Condon's fighter began to trail smoke soon after attacking the train. Despite his attempts to exit the stricken fighter, Condon perished when the Lightning dived into the ground and exploded from a height of 2000 ft (*via William Hess*)

rout a powerful enemy formation. And, conversely, have seen flights lose their advantage through hesitation. Obviously, aggression can be carried to the point of foolhardiness. However, this sort of action is never so foolish as poking around looking for an ideal set-up, and ending up by being jumped yourself.

The Japanese pilot, in general, is not aggressive, but I wouldn't accept this as a hard and fast rule, for every tenth pilot you run into tries to do just that. It is extremely unwise to consider the Japanese pilots as not good. If you are unfortunate enough to have one on your tail, it is my opinion that a positive change in direction is your best evasive manoeuvre. Don't ever think a straight and level skid will help him miss. He isn't too good a shot, but he'll like that. Do something quick that will make him need a lead to hit you.

Up to the present operation, our missions were averaging around seven hours of flying. For these missions it is necessary for each pilot to know, unequivocally, the maximum performance of his aeroplane. It is more important for a fighter pilot in the SWPA to know how to get the most distance and the most time from his gasoline than to know the minimum speed from which he can do an Immelman.

Of course, a good fighter pilot should know everything, far from the least of which is how to shoot. Never fire long bursts. This procedure not

Lt Col MacDonald flies his natural metal P-38J-15 over the Markham Valley in the spring of 1944. The Erap River, seen off to the left of the Lightning, flowed straight through the 475th FG's new base at Nadzab (*via John Stanaway*)

Charles H MacDonald

Charles Henry 'Mac' MacDonald was born on 23 November 1915 in Dubois, Pennsylvania. He revealed an interest in aeronautics and flying during his high school years, although he actually studied philosophy at Louisiana State University. Upon his graduation in 1938, MacDonald was accepted into the US Army Air Corps' flying cadet programme for reservists, and he undertook his flying training at Kelly Field, in Texas, between 29 June 1938 and 25 May 1939. The following month he was sent to the 20th PG's 79th PS, which had been the first unit in the Air Corps to swap its P-26 'Peashooters' for P-36A Hawks. His stay with the group, based in Barksdale, Louisiana, only lasted a matter of months, for MacDonald was posted to the 21st PS/35th PG upon its formation at Moffett Field, California, on 1 February 1940. Here, he again flew the P-36A, and during his time with the unit he was transferred to the Air Corps on a permanent commission (on 9 September 1940).

Four of the key personalities in the 475th FG in the summer of 1944 pose for a group photograph at Biak. They are, from left to right, Maj 'Tommy' McGuire (431st FS CO), Charles Lindbergh, Lt Col Meryl Smith (475th FG Ops Officer) and Col Charles MacDonald, 475th FG CO). Smith would assume command of the group on 4 August 1944 when MacDonald was temporarily grounded for 60 days and sent home on leave after letting civilian Lindbergh see combat on a number of missions – he shot down a Ki-51 'Sonia' reconnaissance aircraft during one such sortie! Promoted to lieutenant colonel, Smith was killed in combat with Japanese naval fighters over Ormoc Bay on 7 December 1944, the veteran pilot having downed two 'Jacks' just minutes prior to his death (*via John Stanaway*)

MacDonald then joined yet another newly formed squadron when he was sent to the 70th PS/55th PG at Hamilton Field, in California, on 15 January 1941. He briefly flew the rare P-43 Lancer with this squadron until being sent to the 44th PS/18th PG at Wheeler Field, in Hawaii, just 25 days after arriving at Hamilton Field! Soon after his arrival, the 18th replaced its P-36As with P-40Bs, and during the attack on Pearl Harbor on 7 December 1941, he managed to get a damaged Curtiss fighter airborne and patrol the western side of the island. However, his biggest enemy was the flak from nervous gunners, as the Japanese aircraft had already returned to their respective carriers by the time he started his search.

Promoted to captain on 1 March 1942 and then major on 10 October that same year, MacDonald returned to the United States, where he undertook conversion training onto the P-47 with the 326th FG. He was then posted to the newly formed 348th FG at Westover Field, Massachusetts, on 17 November 1942, becoming CO of its 340th FS. MacDonald remained in charge of the unit until 1 October 1943, by which time it had been well and truly 'blooded' in combat over New Guinea. He was then posted to the Lightning-equipped 475th FG at Dobodura as group executive officer.

Having not scored a single kill with the P-47D in over three months of combat, MacDonald enjoyed immediate success with the P-38H, claiming four victories over Oro Bay and Rabaul on 15 (two 'Vals'), 23 (an 'Oscar') and 25 October (a 'Zeke'). He 'made ace' (in P-38H-5 42-66846) near Alexishafen airfield on 9 November when he destroyed two more 'Zekes', and was rewarded for his efforts with a promotion to lieutenant colonel the following day. On 26 November MacDonald became CO of the 475th FG, and he would remain in charge until August 1944. He finished off a memorable year with two 'Vals' destroyed over Arawe on 21 December, and then claimed a further two victories in January 1944 (a 'Tony' on the 10th and a 'Hamp' on the 18th) over Wewak. The Japanese had taken such a beating in late 1943 and early 1944 that few aircraft were encountered by prowling V Fighter Command fighters during the summer, and MacDonald – who was made a full colonel in May – had to wait until 8 June to claim his next victory (a 'Zeke'). He then destroyed a rare A6M2-N 'Rufe' seaplane fighter and a 'Val' on 1 August near Koror Island.

MacDonald was posted home on leave three days after claiming this victory, numerous post-war historians stating that he was sent on a '60-day pass' as punishment for letting legendary civilian pilot Charles Lindbergh see combat (and claim an aerial kill) during his time 'advising' the 475th FG in June-July 1944. MacDonald returned to the SWPA, and leadership of the group, just in time to participate in the long-range sweeps of the Philippines as part of the prelude to invasion. These missions provoked an upswing in Japanese fighter activity, and between 10 November 1944 and 1 January 1945, MacDonald claimed 13 kills flying a brand new P-38L-1. Having boosted his score to 26 victories, MacDonald scored his final kill – a lone Ki-57 'Topsy' transport – on 13 February during a low-level fighter sweep of Indochina.

'Mac' MacDonald left the 475th FG in June 1945, and remaining in the Army Air Force post-war, he served as the Legislative Liaison to the House Armed Services Committee in Washington, DC until mid-1948. Graduating from the Air War College at Maxwell Air Force Base in 1949, MacDonald's later assignments included time as CO of the F-84-equipped 33rd FG at Otis Field, Massachusetts, Operations Officer at the 1st Air Force Headquarters, Mitchell Field, and Commander of the 23rd FW, flying F-86 Sabres, at Presque Isle, Maine. MacDonald next served as the Air Attaché to Sweden for three years, and then in 1956 began a three-year tour, first as a student and then as an instructor, at the National War College in Fort McNair. His last assignment was as the Deputy Commander of the 25th Air Division at McChord Air Force Base, Washington.

Something of a nonconformist, 'Mac' MacDonald retired from the USAF in 1961 and spent the next ten years touring the Pacific and the Caribbean in his yacht until he ended up in Costa Rica. In the final years of his life he lived simply in the wilds of Florida with his beloved animals, until passing away on 4 March 2002.

The fourth *PUTT PUTT MARU* (P-38L-5 44-25643) has Col MacDonald's 26 victory flags applied at Dulag, on Leyte, in early January 1945. This aircraft replaced 44-24843, which was lost in combat on 2 January. 44-25643 survived less than a month in the frontline, however, for it is listed as having been written off in a taxiing accident on 27 January after it had been passed on to Maj John Loisel (*via John Stanaway*)

only wastes ammunition, but heats the guns to the point where the bullets lose speed and direction.

With the new aeroplanes our enemy is developing, and the psychological effect of fighting closer to his home land, I do not doubt that we will have to revise our opinions and our tactics.

MAJ JOHN S LOISEL
OPERATIONS OFFICER
475th FG

Aggressiveness is a quality which must be possessed by every fighter pilot. It is the aggressive pilot who gives, not receives, the punishment. A good combat outfit will not coddle the weak pilot, but will build a strong fighting machine around pilots who have confidence in the aeroplanes they fly and in themselves. The importance of teamwork in aerial combat cannot be over-emphasised. If teamwork is to be achieved, and the effects of mutual support gained, each flight leader must know the position of every man in his flight. This is possible only when strict formation discipline is observed at all times. I prefer to have my wingman at a distance of about 100 yards, and at a 45-degree angle to the rear. In combat, he will be more in trail and at a distance of ten ship lengths behind me.

The leader's primary objective is to shoot down the enemy – it is the wingman's responsibility to stick with him, and at the same time be on the lookout for possible attackers. The wingman constitutes the defensive part of the unit, and his primary responsibility is the protection of that unit. I do not believe in breaking up the basic four-ship flight, and definitely never less than two-ships together. Flight leaders should position their flights close enough to the lead flight to be able to effectively support any attack or defensive manoeuvres.

In entering combat, hit the enemy with everything you've got. The initial attack will generally govern the outcome of the fight. A piecemeal entry into the scrap will not be as effective as several flights hitting the enemy simultaneously. Head for the main body of the enemy if you are leading a flight or a squadron. Disregard the stragglers. In my experience at hitting enemy formations, a few wingmen have seen me coming and have taken evasive action, but where the enemy was most concentrated, there were several who obviously didn't know of our presence.

I well remember one incident in which the squadron leader first turned to pick up the highest stragglers of a large group of Japanese fighters. This gave the main body of the enemy the opportunity to gain superior altitude advantage, which they utilised by positioning themselves on our tails.

Plough into the largest bunch you see. After such an attack the enemy will be forced to break up. Stay together as a squadron as long as the enemy maintains a semblance of large flights. If he breaks up into singles and elements you can best cope with him by breaking down into flights. Always maintain a numerical superiority in size of formations involved and it will pay dividends. Elements are completely satisfactory for attacking singles or other elements, but in a general melee, as most fights turn out to be, you must always be prepared to contact a larger enemy group.

432nd FS CO Capt John Loisel (second from right) enjoys a cigarette in front of his P-38H-1 42-66682 at Dobodura in late January 1944. Standing at the extreme left is Loisel's crew chief, T/Sgt K E Lawrence, whilst the CO himself is flanked by two unnamed squadron pilots. Loisel claimed as many as four of his eleven kills in this aircraft, which he christened *SCREAMIN' KID*. P-38s would typically survive less than six months in the frontline with V Fighter Command, but 42-66682 remained in service with the 475th FG for more than eight (*via John Stanaway*)

In one particular instance, I chased a flight of six enemy fighters with just my element, and was promptly chased out of the fight for my pains.

Knowledge of the manoeuvrability limits of your ship enables you to figure out just how long you can turn with the enemy in a pass. The new P-38Ls we are getting have better manoeuvring characteristics than any previous P-38 model, but the enemy can still out-manoeuvre any fighter we have. Dive flaps do not increase your rate of turn. Some fellows have been throwing them down after rolling into a turn and, because back pressure on the controls is decreased, they falsely imagine they're pulling their nose through faster.

Superior speed is still our greatest advantage. Come down on the enemy, if possible, attack him level, but NEVER make a climbing pass on his fighters without lots of speed. When you zoom, turn or slow up in anyway you are especially vulnerable.

The long-range operations of the past nine months have increased the fighter pilot's problems many times. Knowing your aeroplane, and its possibilities and operation under all conditions, will greatly help. Too many pilots do not know how to get maximum performance out of their aircraft and engines. Just as an example, on very long missions we had trouble at first getting pilots to use 1600 RPM and 28 to 32 inches of manifold pressure. They'd been accustomed to using 2100 to 2300 RPM for the same manifold pressures, not knowing that the P-38 operating instructions gave the lower figures for maximum gas economy.

Always press your attacks closely. Don't waste ammunition or give away your attack until you are within effective range. Shots, especially those half-hearted out of range snapshots so many of us take, are particularly useless. Never turn with the enemy. If you can't hold your lead on

This unidentified P-38L-5 was Lt Col John Loisel's mount at war's end, its 'blue 100' denoting his position as group CO. He took over command of the 475th FG from Col MacDonald on 14 July 1945, and remained group CO until 18 April 1946. This photograph was taken at Ie Shima (*via John Stanaway*)

Having gained valuable combat experience flying Airacobras with the 8th FG in the SWPA in 1942, John Loisel was handpicked to join the all new 475th FG in June 1943 (*via John Stanaway*)

him, break away. Your greatest assets are speed and firepower. When you are not using one, use the other.

When you are leading a flight or a squadron, your problems are multiplied – if covering bombers, your responsibility extends to them. If you can maintain radio discipline and formation, and everyone knows what you are expecting of them, your problem is greatly reduced. As soon as the enemy

John S Loisel

John Simon Loisel was born on 21 May 1920 in Coeur d'Alene, Idaho. He attended Wayne State Teachers' College (Nebraska) and the University of Nebraska from 1938 to 1941, when he joined the Army Reserves. Loisel undertook flying training at Mather Field, California, from 10 March to 31 October 1941, and upon graduation became an instructor with the Army Air Corps. He was eventually posted to the 36th FS/8th FG in New Guinea in September 1942, and flew 83 combat missions with the unit in the P-39D and P-400.

Loisel remained with the 8th FG until June 1943, when he was handpicked, along with a host of other talented V Fighter Command pilots, to form the 475th FG at Amberley Field in Queensland, Australia. The unit was equipped with P-38H Lightnings, and Loisel assigned to the group's 432nd FS. Moving to Dobodura, New Guinea, in August, Loisel wasted not time in opening his score with the Lockheed fighter when he claimed two 'Tonys' shot down during the course of a bomber escort mission to Wewak on 21 August. He then destroyed a 'Zeke' near Finschhafen on 22 September, and followed this up with two more 'Zekes' over Oro Bay on 15 October to gain ace status. Three days later he was promoted to captain. Loisel's final kills in 1943 came on 13 and 21 December, when he again downed two more 'Zekes' in the build up to the Operation *Alamo* landings on Cape Gloucester.

is sighted, the squadron goes into string formation ten ship lengths between aeroplanes. Stay together and don't allow stragglers. In a string formation, the flights can weave and cross, meeting any attack. If with bombers, speed can be maintained, and yet stay with them by weaving.

In very rare instances does a good squadron get jumped. Keep looking around and be ready for a fight at all times. When tackling an enemy formation, try to achieve the element of surprise, but don't forget speed and firepower are still your greatest assets.

When enemy fighters are scarce and the missions call for strafing and dive-bombing, don't relax the discipline of your outfit. Keep up the spirit and teamwork by never allowing sloppy formations, patterns or a low calibre of flying. Give every flight everything you've got and it will pay dividends in combat.

MAJ THOMAS B McGUIRE JR
431st FS/475th FG

To completely cover fighter tactics in a single letter would be impossible, but I would like to give a resume of my views on combat tactics – both

On 22 January 1944 John Loisel was made CO of the 432nd FS, and one of his first priorities as the new boss was to raise the proficiency of his pilots in 90-degree deflection shooting, thus preventing them from 'spraying lead all over the air'. Proving that he had mastered the technique, Loisel destroyed a 'Zeke' just 24 hours after becoming CO of the unit. Over the next few weeks the 475th flew numerous strike missions against targets in New Guinea and the Halmaharas, and on 3 April Loisel shot down an 'Oscar' and a 'Hamp' during a low-level bomber escort mission against enemy airfields at Hollandia, New Guinea. By then his unit had re-equipped with the latest P-38J-15 version of the Lightning. Promoted to major in late April, Loisel returned home on leave on 4 August.

The ten-kill ace returned to the Pacific in January 1945, rejoining the 475th FG as group operations officer. Flying P-38L-5s from the Philippines, Loisel claimed his final kill on 28 March 1945 when he destroyed a Ki-84 'Frank' near Tre Island, off Indochina. Promoted to lieutenant colonel on 15 May, he assumed command of the 475th on 15 July and led the group to Ie Shima, on Okinawa, and then onto Kimpo, in Korea, post-war. He relinquished command on 18 April 1946 and returned home, having flown 301 operational missions in the SWPA.

Going back to his studies in the late 1940s, Loisel graduated from the University of Nebraska with a degree in physics in 1949. Promoted to full colonel on 1 December 1951, he returned to combat in Korea in May 1953 when he was made commander of the 474th Fighter Bomber Group, which was flying ground attack missions in the F-84 from Taegu. Retiring from the USAF in 1970, he earned a masters degree from the North Texas State University two years later and then taught in Plano (Texas) high schools until retiring in 1985.

The 475th FG's ranking ace 'Tommy' McGuire flew at least five P-38s named *PUDGY* (after his fiancee) during his time in the SWPA. This particular machine was P-38H-5 42-66817, which was his second assigned Lightning. He used it to destroy three 'Vals' over Cape Gloucester on 26 December 1943, raising his tally to 17 victories. This photograph was taken at Dobodura soon after McGuire had enjoyed his Boxing Day success. There is a colour profile of this machine on page 76 (*via John Stanaway*)

individual and squadron – based on my extensive personal combat experience in the SWPA.

On the missions we have been flying for the past few months, gas economy has been a paramount consideration. Gas economy should always be practiced, but on long-range missions it becomes essential to save gas. We have found that a combination of low RPM and corresponding high manifold pressure (i.e. 1600 RPM – 32 inches HG) going to and from the target will give maximum miles per gallon. If you are to have sufficient gas to cover the bombers clear of the target, and also have sufficient reserve for weather, gas economy must be practiced. Rendezvous points should be as close to the target as is tactically practical.

On individual combat tactics, aggressiveness is the keynote of success. A fighter pilot must be aggressive. The enemy on the defensive gives you the advantage, as he is trying to evade you, and not to shoot you down. Never break your formation into less than two-ship elements. Stay in pairs. A man by himself is a liability, but a two-ship team is an asset. If you are separated, join up immediately with other friendly aeroplanes. On the defensive, keep up your speed. A shallow, high-speed dive or climb is your best evasive action against a stern attack. You must never reverse your turn – that is asking for it. Try to make the enemy commit himself, then turn into his attack. If forced to turn, go to the right if possible.

On the offensive, break up the enemy's formation. If you can scatter and split up your foe, they will be unable to press an attack on the bombers and will also be unable to give support to each other when in trouble. Don't turn with the enemy. It can't be done.

Your main assets are speed and firepower – use them. Press your attacks close-in to a minimum range. Go in close, and then when you think you are too close, go on in closer.

Legendary transatlantic solo pilot Charles Lindbergh and 475th FG 'ace of aces' 'Tommy' McGuire enjoyed a sparky relationship during the former's two-month spell with the group in the summer of 1944. Lindbergh was in the SWPA as a representative of the United Aircraft Corporation, and having spent time improving the range and performance of Marine F4U Corsairs (manufactured by United), he had requested a transfer to a Lightning unit to see whether he could also boost the Lockheed fighter's performance. Once with the 475th FG, he asked to fly on combat missions in order see where improvements could be made, and Maj McGuire agreed to take him on his wing. According to eyewitnesses, the two pilots often verbally sparred with each other when out of the cockpit, McGuire persistently taunting Lindbergh and making him do small favours, knowing full well that the latter could not retaliate due to his tenuous guest status. Lindbergh was an incorrigible practical joker, however, and routinely got his own back on an unsuspecting McGuire (*via William Hess*)

At minimum range your shots count, and there is less chance of missing your target. On deflection shots, pull your sight through the target. Most shots in deflection are missed by being over or under rather than by incorrect lead. Never turn with a foe past the point where you can't hold your lead. Don't let the enemy trick you into pulling up or turning until you lose your speed. Always clear yourself before and during an attack. It is always the one you don't see that gets you. On long range missions especially, don't chase a single out of the fight – he is probably trying to lure you away from the scrap. Your job is to provide cover for the bombers, and you reduce the effectiveness of your squadron if you get sucked out of the fight.

Squadron formation multiplies your problems. You not only have to think of yourself, but also of 15 men behind you. The squadron commander's responsibility lies not only to his own formation, but also to

P-38J-15 *PUDGY III* (serial unknown) was 'Tommy' McGuire's assigned machine for much of the spring and summer of 1944. This photograph was taken at Biak soon after it had been used to claim McGuire's 21st kill. Note the squadron commander's twin vertical stripes forward of the tail (*via William Hess*)

Thomas B McGuire Jr

Thomas Buchanan 'Tommy' McGuire was born in Ridgewood, New Jersey, on 1 August 1920. Enrolling in the mechanical engineering course at the Georgia School of Technology in 1937, his interest in aviation first surfaced in 1940 when he learned to fly the Piper Cub at nearby Candler Field. McGuire then decided that military flying was for him, and he dropped out of school in July 1941 and enlisted in the Army Reserves as an aviation cadet. He completed his training as part of Class 42-B at Kelly Field, in Texas, on 2 February 1942 and was posted to the 50th PG/313th PS at Key Field, Mississippi, three months later. Flying antiquated P-35s, he asked for overseas duty and was posted to the P-39F-equipped 56th PS/54th PG in the Aleutians. Weather was the greatest enemy facing fighter pilots in this 'forgotten' theatre, and McGuire soon wanted out. Returning to the USA in mid October, he converted onto the P-38 and was sent to the 9th FS/49th FG in March 1943.

'Tommy' failed to score whilst flying with this group, and it was not until he transferred to the newly formed 431st FS/475th FG that he began to make his mark. He claimed his first victories (two 'Zekes' and a 'Tony') on 18 August over Wewak during his first encounter with the enemy, and followed this up with two more 'Zekes' in the same area three days later to 'make ace'. McGuire ended the month with a further two kills (a 'Zeke' and a 'Tony') on the 29th, again over Wewak. He would remain in the thick of the action for the rest of the year, scoring two kills in September, four in October (he was also shot down and wounded on the 17th of this month, but not before first destroying three 'Zekes') and three in December.

Promoted to captain in late 1943, McGuire was obsessed with becoming the first American pilot to surpass Capt Eddie Rickenbacker's World War 1 tally of 26 kills. However, he was sent home on leave in early 1944, and this allowed his great rival Dick Bong to better Rickenbacker's score on 12 April. McGuire returned to the SWPA in May 1944, where he was promoted to major and made CO of the 431st FS. He soon began making up for lost time, claiming two kills before month-end, two more in June and then a solitary victory in July. The Japanese had suffered terrible losses both on the ground and in the air in New Guinea, and few enemy aircraft were to be encountered by V Fighter Command until it started sending groups on long-range fighter sweeps over the Philippines and Borneo in October. More lengthy missions followed

This rare shot of a smiling Maj Tom McGuire shows him devoid of his distinctively battered service cap, which was a permanent fixture atop his head when the 'Iron Major' was not flying (*via William Hess*)

in November, as the 475th went in search of Japanese fighters in the prelude to the invasion of Leyte and Cebu.

Fixated with matching Dick Bong's tally, McGuire aggressively sought out the enemy during these sweeps, claiming three kills (an 'Oscar', a 'Hamp' and a 'Tojo') on 14 October whilst escorting B-24s sent to bomb the oil refineries at Balikpapan, on Borneo. Four more victories would come the way of the group's leading ace in November as he pushed past Eddie Rickenbacker's 26-kill mark and set off after Bong. By the end of the month, the latter pilot had 36

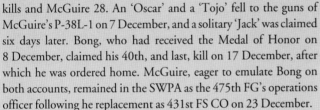

"Pudgy IV" is yet another V Fighter Command mystery machine, being used by Maj McGuire in the late summer of 1944. Photographed at Biak, it boasts 22 victory flags (*via John Stanaway*)

kills and McGuire 28. An 'Oscar' and a 'Tojo' fell to the guns of McGuire's P-38L-1 on 7 December, and a solitary 'Jack' was claimed six days later. Bong, who had received the Medal of Honor on 8 December, claimed his 40th, and last, kill on 17 December, after which he was ordered home. McGuire, eager to emulate Bong on both accounts, remained in the SWPA as the 475th FG's operations officer following he replacement as 431st FS CO on 23 December.

Freed of the responsibility of leading a unit, McGuire now made sure that he was on those missions deemed most likely to encounter the enemy, whose presence in the air was becoming rarer by the day. On 25 and 26 December McGuire enjoyed his best 48 hours in combat, claiming no fewer than seven 'Zekes' to boost his tally to 38 kills. However, these would prove to be his last victories, for on 7 January 1945 he was to lose his life in combat flying an unauthorised sweep over Los Negros Island. The mission had been specially staged to push his score past 40 victories, and McGuire was trying to manoeuvre in behind a lone Ki-43 just above the tree-tops when his fighter – still carrying its near-full long-range external tanks – snap-rolled onto its back and crashed into the jungle. 'Tommy' McGuire died instantly.

America's second-ranking ace received a posthumous Medal of Honor on 7 March 1946, and in January 1948 Fort Dix Field, in New Jersey, was renamed McGuire Air Force Base in his honour.

A controversial figure who polarised the men that flew with him, 'Tommy' McGuire's personality and leadership styles have often been commented on in the decades since his death. 'He was an extremely ambitious man. He worked hard, and that's why he got to be squadron commander. He was more a great leader of men in the air than on the ground', commented McGuire's immediate boss (and third-ranking P-38 ace), Col Charles MacDonald, who commanded the 475th FG for much of the time that 'Tommy' was CO of the 431st FS. Another who remarked on the P-38 ace's qualities was 433rd FS pilot Carroll Anderson. 'McGuire was an earthy type of guy who led by example. And although he could be abrasive and caustic, he fought and led from the front'.

the bombers he is covering. Radio control by the squadron commander can be had only if the men in the formation keep their radio conversation to an absolute minimum. I like the squadron to drop from escort formation to string formation as soon as the enemy is sighted. We use a string of flights made up of four-ship components. Each man should be back six to ten ship lengths, with an interval about double that between flights. In a fight, outside of the first pass, the flights are independent in picking their targets, staying of course in the same general area. No flight should chase enemy aircraft out of the fight unless the enemy has been split up and is leaving the vicinity.

When the squadron is on the defensive, stay together. Don't allow stragglers. Keep up the flights, and have them weave and cross. An attack from any point can be turned into and broken up. Your men must look around – there is no excuse for a squadron being jumped and surprised if everyone does his job. Almost every one of our losses are ships straggling on their own. A squadron that keeps up its speed, stays together and fights as a team will lose very few men.

On the offensive, whether attacking bombers or fighters, or defending your own bombers against enemy fighters, be aggressive. Break up the Japanese formation, as that is half your battle. Once the enemy is broken up he becomes disorganised and loses all semblance of mutual support. When attacking bomber formations, make your attack, if possible, from 45 degrees head-on, coming in as close as possible and passing within 50 ft of the bombers, then passing over or under them, before breaking your pass. This will break up the formation, enabling you to break into flights to go after pairs and individual ships.

When covering bombers, if it is possible, don't wait for the enemy attack. Take your squadron into the thickest bunch and split them up. Fight over the bombers as long as possible. You will not only prevent most attacks, but also those that get through will expose themselves to you. A fighter is most vulnerable when making an attack. A fighter pilot must live up to what his name implies. You must be aggressive to do your job.

CAPT ELLIOT SUMMER
432nd FS/475th FG

In reply to your recent letter concerning the tactics we use in this theatre, the following is submitted.

INDIVIDUAL COMBAT TACTICS

A defensive element should be about a quarter-mile to the side (of the bombers), with wingmen about 75 yards behind their respective leaders. A speed of at least 250 mph should be maintained at all times – the faster the better. This formation, by using mutual support, can ward off all types of attack.

If you are found alone, join with other P-38s at once. If caught by the enemy, and you have plenty of altitude, the trick of chopping one throttle and applying aileron and rudder will lose him.

Always try to maintain four-ship flights and at all times. Escort a P-38 on a single engine.

432nd FS pilot 1Lt Elliot Summer was assigned unknown P-38H-5 *BLOOD & GUTS III* in late 1943, and he scored possibly as many as three kills with it in December of that year (*via William Hess*)

When on the offensive, employ the same string formation as mentioned above, but with more flexibility. The element leader may lead the attack if better positioned.

When out-numbering the enemy, elements may break, but in doing so, the wingmen move farther out to the side to provide mutual protection while attacking.

You will close fast on the enemy, as he is usually flitting around at 180 to 220 mph. Get in close enough to see his teeth before firing. The wingman can usually get a good shot by dropping below the leader and catching the enemy as he tries to 'split-S'.

SQUADRON FORMATION COMBAT TACTICS

When leading and controlling the unit, radio transmission and reception is of the utmost importance. Air discipline must never be relaxed to insure each pilot reacts correctly in all circumstances. Confidence in the leader's ability and judgement must be maintained by all pilots.

When flying defensively, the squadron consists of four flights – Red, White, Blue and Green – flying in a diamond formation. White flight flies on the right flank, slightly below and behind Red flight. Blue flies left flank, above Red and behind White. Green flight flies directly behind Red. The altitude difference between the low flight and top flight is not more than 1500 ft. The space between flanks is about three-quarters of a mile. This provides for maximum visibility and protection. When attacked, Red and White provide mutual protection, as do Blue and Green.

When flying offensively, the diamond formation remains the same, with the flights taking up their offensive strings. This formation is very flexible, allowing each of the flight leaders to use his initiative. The flights may separate when outnumbering the enemy, but otherwise stay in the same area to provide mutual protection.

TACTICS PROBABLE WITH P-38L AND G-SUIT

This combination makes possible many new tactics both offensively and defensively. The G-suit, aileron boost and dive brakes allow for very

121

high-speed dives, tight turns, abrupt pull-outs and a high rate of roll. I found it impossible for me to black out, although I indicated 575 mph, dropped dive flaps and reefed in as tight as possible. The pull-out was so severe as to buckle the wings.

There is a possibility that at speeds of around 300 mph, the combination of G-suit and P-38L would allow for turning with the enemy. One thing is certain. Rolls and tight turns when done at indicated airspeeds of 300 mph and over cannot be followed by any Japanese aeroplane thus far encountered in this theatre.

Elliot Summer

Elliott Summer was born on 22 November 1919 in Providence, Rhode Island. He was studying architecture at Columbia University when he volunteered for service with the US Army Air Corps. Graduating from flight training at Luke Field, Arizona, on 4 January 1943, Summer was then sent to the 360th FG at Glendale, in California, to conduct his transition training onto the P-38. His final conversion training was carried out with the co-located 329th FG, and on 23 July he was one of the few 'nugget' pilots assigned to the newly formed 432nd FS/475th FG in Amberley, Queensland.

On 14 August the group moved north to Dobodura, in New Guinea, and Summer claimed his first kill exactly one week later when he downed a 'Zeke' near Dagua in P-38H-1 42-66575. He scored two further victories in October, destroying an 'Oscar' on the 15th and another Ki-43 on the 24th. Summer achieved ace status on 21 December when he downed two 'Val' dive-bombers over Arawe, and he followed this up with a single 'Zeke' over Wewak the following day. Almost four months would pass before he claimed his next victory, by which time the 432nd FS had swapped its war-weary H-model Lightnings for new P-38J-15s. Summer claimed a Ki-43 (also listed as a 'Zeke') while escorting A-20s and B-25s sent to bomb Hollandia on 3 April 1944. Japanese aircraft then effectively disappeared from the skies over New Guinea, as the theatre was effectively cut off from Japan by the allied 'island hopping' campaign elsewhere in the Pacific.

Like most V Fighter Command pilots in the SWPA, Summer would add further kills to his tally during fighter sweeps of the Philippines in late 1944, the ace destroying two 'Zekes' over Tacloban Bay on 12 November and an 'Oscar' over Ormoc Bay on 7 December. Promoted to captain in the autumn of 1944, Summer became CO of the 432nd FS on 2 January 1945, and he remained in command until the end of July, when he was posted back to the United States. Post-war, he entered government service, becoming a noise abatement officer for the Federal Aviation Administration.

One of the few 'nugget' pilots assigned to the 475th FG upon its formation in Australia in 1943, Elliot Summer learned quickly from the various combat veterans that made up the bulk of the group's flying staff. He was an ace by Christmas 1943, and ended the war with ten kills to his name (*via William Hess*)

APPENDICES

COLOUR PLATES

1

P-47D-3 42-22604 of 1Lt William Giroux, 36th FS/8th FG, Port Moresby, late November 1943

Future ten-kill ace 'Kenny' Giroux lodged his first aerial claims whilst flying this machine on the morning of 7 November 1943 when he probably destroyed a trio of Ki-21 'Sally' bombers over Nadzab. A lack of independent corroboration for these claims resulted in Giroux being credited with three probables only, although he optimistically adorned his fighter with two victory decals (on both sides of the fuselage). These were his only successes with the Thunderbolt. The 36th FS received its first P-47s as replacements for its war-weary P-39s and P-400s in late October 1943, and by the end of the following month the unit had completed its transition to the Republic fighter. Giroux, who professed a liking for the P-47 post-war, had his machine adorned with the letter 'G', for obvious reasons. Aside from the theatre-standard all-white tail surfaces and wing leading edges, the 36th FS was almost certainly unique in painting the engine cowling flaps this colour as well.

2

P-38J-15 (serial unknown) of 1Lt William Giroux, 36th FS/ 8th FG, Owi (Schouten Islands), early September 1944

'Kenny' Giroux had added two confirmed kills to his probables by September 1944, his unit having parted with its Thunderbolts for a batch of decidedly secondhand P-38Hs in early March 1944. These machines were in turn replaced with much fresher P-38Js during the summer, this particular machine being issued to Giroux. He added various personal touches to his Lightning, and it is presumed that the original WHILMA was one of the veteran P-38Hs initially supplied to the 36th FS. Giroux almost certainly used this J-15 to claim a Ki-43 destroyed on 27 July and to damage a Ki-48 'Lily' light bomber on 2 September. The puppy motif was present on both engines, and the name *Dead Eye Daisy* appeared on the starboard side of the nose. Black-striped spinners and white fin tips were the unit markings adopted by the 36th FS following the squadron's switch to the P-38.

3

P-38J-20 44-23255 of Capt William Giroux, 36th FS/ 8th FG, San Jose (Mindoro), January 1945

'Kenny' Giroux really hit his straps as a fighter pilot during the retaking of the Philippines in late 1944, claiming eight kills between 2 and 15 November. His victims were all fighter aircraft, and they almost certainly fell to the guns of this particular P-38J-20. Devoid of personal embellishment bar the pilot's name and scoreboard, the Lightning featured the revised 36th FS markings – namely thicker spinner stripes and new black and white diagonal wing stripes.

4

P-38G-1 42-12705 of 1Lt Cy Homer, 80th FS/8th FG, Port Moresby, November 1943

This particular P-38G-1 was the first Lightning assigned to 15-kill ace Cy Homer upon his arrival in the Southwest Pacific, the fighter having been supplied new to the 80th FS when the unit transitioned from the P-39 onto the Lockheed fighter in Queensland, Australia, in early 1943. Variously named *COTTON DUSTER*, *AVA* and *LILLY NELL* by its pilot and groundcrew, the Lightning was routinely flown by Homer throughout 1943 – a remarkably long period for a frontline fighter in the SWPA. Indeed, he claimed two kills and three probables with 42-12705 between 21 May and 7 November. Homer's remaining victories (three) for 1943 were scored in P-38G-15 43-2386 on 21 August.

5

P-38J (serial unknown) of Capt Cy Homer, CO of the 80th FS/8th FG, Morotai, November 1944

Cy Homer enjoyed significant success in the air during the first half of 1944, claiming nine kills, two probables and three damaged between 18 January and 27 July – all were fighters. More than half of these victories were scored in a P-38J-15, although unit records are not detailed enough to denote exactly what aircraft Homer was flying for any of these kills. Photographic evidence proves that he was regularly flying this machine from Morotai in the autumn of 1944, the fighter featuring 16 victory decals below the cockpit – Homer was in fact only credited with 15 confirmed kills. Soon after being made CO of the 80th FS on 4 October, Homer used the privilege of rank to have the tail surfaces of *UNCLE CY'S Angel* painted in green and white checks!

6

P-38J-10 42-67898 of 1Lt Allen Hill, 80th FS/8th FG, Finschhafen, January 1944

The female form has always proven popular with American pilots in combat, and the appeal of a scantily clad woman proved irresistible to Allen Hill. Issued with one of the first P-38J-10s supplied to the 80th FS, he had the fighter adorned with at least two *HILL's Angels* – only the one on the port side was actually clothed! Hill almost certainly claimed his sixth kill (a Ki-61) in this aircraft on 18 January 1944.

7

P-38J (serial unknown) of Capt Allen Hill, 80th FS/8th FG, Morotai, autumn 1944

Very little is known about this machine other than the fact that it bore Allen Hill's 'H' letter code and the *HILL'S Angels* titling on the nose. It also featured the 80th FS green and white unit markings on the propeller spinners and vertical tail

123

surfaces. It was almost certainly the last P-38J assigned to Hill prior to his posting to the 36th FS as unit CO in mid November 1944.

8

P-47D-23 42-278?? of Capt Leroy Grossheusch, CO of the 39th FS/35th FG, Mangaldan (Luzon), February 1945

This colourful P-47D-23 was almost certainly issued to Capt Leroy Grossheusch in June 1944, and it remained assigned to him until well into 1945. The eight-kill ace adorned all of his fighters with the number 33, and he almost certainly claimed six of his eight victories in this veteran machine between 30 January and 25 February 1945. Note the blue diagonal command stripes painted beneath the cockpit. Flight leaders' aircraft boasted a single stripe in this location.

9

P-51D-20 44-64124 of Capt Leroy Grossheusch, CO of the 39th FS/35th FG, Okinawa, August 1945

Grossheusch claimed his final victory (a Ki-84 'Frank') in this machine on 12 August 1945 during a long range sweep of the Japanese home islands. Marked in the 39th FS's distinctive blue squadron colours, the aircraft was named *Little Girl* by its pilot. This was Grossheusch's second Mustang, as he had written his first P-51D off on 30 July 1945 attacking a Japanese destroyer near the naval base of Goto Retto, in southern Japan. He had struck the ship's waterline with a long burst of 0.50-cal machine gun fire, and a number of the rounds had penetrated the hull into the magazine. 'There was a terrific explosion', Grossheusch later recalled. 'A huge, gigantic ball of fire which I had to fly through because I was too close to avoid it. One of the guys in the flight said, "What the hell was that?" Another voice said, "I think Lee dove into the destroyer". By then, my heart had gotten out of my throat so I told them that I was okay, but damaged. I had sunk the destroyer, but my poor P-51 was so riddled with shrapnel and debris from the explosion that it had to be scrapped once we got back to Okinawa'.

10

P-38H-1 (serial unknown) of Capt Gerald Johnson, CO of the 9th FS/49th FG, Dobodura, November 1943

P-38H-1 '83' was inherited by 'Jerry' Johnson when he replaced future ETO 'ace-in-a-day' Maj Sid Woods as CO of the 9th FS in August 1943. It was marked as aircraft '92' when assigned to Woods, although Johnson soon had this changed to his favoured '83'. Command stripes were also added to the twin tails. He flew this machine on a number of the long range bomber escort missions performed by the 9th FS in support of the Allied bombing campaign against the Japanese stronghold of Rabaul in October-November 1943. These sorties were arduous for both the pilots and their aircraft, and the unit could barely muster 12 serviceable P-38s throughout this period. Nevertheless, 9th FS pilots proved their aerial superiority by downing 22 kills in just four missions – at least three of these fell to Johnson in this very machine.

11

P-47D-5 (serial unknown) of Maj Gerald Johnson, CO of the 9th FS/49th FG, Gusap, January 1944

The 9th FS was forced to part with its beloved P-38s

following the attritional Rabaul campaign, as Lockheed could not supply enough fighters to make good the heavy losses suffered by the 'Flying Knights'. There was no such shortage of P-47s, and the 9th duly converted onto Republic's heavyweight Thunderbolt in late November 1943. Johnson and his men were less than impressed with the P-47D-4, and the 9th FS was the only unit within the 49th FG to fly the fighter. As if to prove their point, only three of the unit's aces scored kills with the P-47, including 'Jerry' Johnson who managed to claim a 'Tony' and a 'Zeke' destroyed in December 1943 and January 1944 respectively. The 9th FS claimed just eight victories in total during its five-month association with the Thunderbolt. Johnson primarily flew this particular machine (serial unknown) up until he was posted home on leave on 29 January 1944, the P-47 featuring his full tally, his favourite side number '83', standard white SWPA identification markings and command stripes.

12

P-38L-5 (serial unknown) of Maj Gerald Johnson, Deputy CO of the 49th FG, Biak (Hollandia), October 1944

This particular aircraft was used by Maj Johnson for much of the Philippines campaign in late 1944, the aircraft featuring no personal markings other than his ever-growing scoreboard and his favourite number '83' on the nose and radiator fairings – this aircraft also featured the number '42' in black on its twin tails at one point. Johnson claimed ten victories between 14 October and 7 December 1944, and some of these kills were almost certainly achieved in this machine.

13

P-40N-5 42-105826 of Maj Gerald Johnson, 49th FG HQ, Biak (Hollandia), October 1944

Upon Johnson's return to the 49th FG from leave in the late summer of 1944, he had been appointed Group Ops Executive. As a perk of the job, he acquired a surplus P-40N that had recently been retired by the group's 7th FS – the latter unit had at last swapped its Warhawks for Lightnings in September 1944. Johnson had the fighter stripped back to bare metal, and had its armament and protective armour removed. The end result was a gleaming, high performance hack that he would regularly use to embarrass novice P-38 pilots in mock dogfights over nearby Sentani Lake.

14

P-38G-5 (serial unknown) of 1Lt Dick Bong, 9th FS/ 49th FG, Dobodura, July 1943

Ranking American ace Dick Bong reportedly used this machine to claim a Ki-43 destroyed northwest of Rein Bay on 28 July 1943 whilst escorting 3rd Air Group B-25s that had been sent to bomb shipping off New Britain and an air strip at Cape Gloucester. A large formations of 'Oscars' had sortied from Rabaul in response to the raid, and the ten 9th FS P-38s and twelve P-39s of the 39th FS were hard-pressed to keep the Japanese fighters away from the B-25s. Nevertheless, the American pilots stuck to their job, and no fewer than seven Ki-43s were claimed to have been destroyed by the P-38s. One of these fell to Dick Bong (for his 16th kill), but not before the upper surface of his left wing had been struck five times by 7.7 mm machine gun rounds fired by a diving 'Oscar'. Bong's P-38 was the only one to be hit in the sortie, and it was duly taken out of service for repairs to be effected. This was possibly the only time he flew 'white 73', for his assigned mount at this time was 'white 79'. Note the white eye motif adorning the engine intake fairing.

15

P-38J-15 42-103993 of Capt Dick Bong, V Fighter Command, Gusap, March 1944

This aircraft was the first of Dick Bong's P-38 to feature the famous portrait of his new sweetheart, Marge Vattendahl, on its nose. He had met his future wife during his extended spell on leave in late 1943. One of the first J-model Lightnings to reach the SWPA, 42-103993 was assigned to Bong following his attachment to V Fighter Command in February 1944. This unique posting suited the young ace perfectly, for he could now pick his missions and fly with any unit he wished in an effort to seek out the enemy. The primary reason for this posting was to ensure that Bong became the first American to pass Eddie Rickenbacker's 26-kill record set in World War 1. Initially flying primarily with the 475th FG, Bong claimed at least three kills with 42-103993 between 15 February and 3 March 1944. The fighter was duly lost in late March when it suffered a mechanical failure whilst being flown by another pilot in bad weather.

16

P-38L-1 44-23964 of Maj Dick Bong, V Fighter Command, Tacloban (Leyte), November 1944

Marked up in 8th FS colours, P-38L-1 44-23964 was Maj Bong's mount during his attachment to the 49th FG as 'gunnery instructor' throughout the Philippines campaign – he had returned to the SWPA in the autumn of 1944 for his third tour, ostensibly in a non-combat role as V Fighter Command's senior gunnery instructor. Sensing the opportunity for more aerial kills with the impending retaking of the Philippines, Bong contacted 49th FG CO Lt Col George Walker and asked him if he could fly attached to his old group for a while. The colonel readily agreed, and commandeered brand new P-38L-1 44-23964 from the 8th FS to serve as Bong's personal mount. The ace would claim six kills with the fighter between 10 October and 11 November 1944, taking his score to 36 victories. 44-23964 was subsequently lost whilst being flown by 49th FG Deputy Ops Officer Maj John Davis on 28 November, the pilot perishing when the fighter stalled in soon after taking off from Tacloban.

17

P-40N-5 (serial unknown, possibly 42-105405) of 1Lt Bob DeHaven, 7th FS/49th FG, Gusap, late January 1944

Bob DeHaven would score ten of his eventual fourteen victories in P-40s of the 7th FS/49th FG, making him equal top of the list of USAAF Warhawk aces in the Pacific theatre. He claimed his first victory in a P-40K on 14 July 1943 and his fifth in this aircraft on 10 December. Like many aircraft in the squadron, it carried different artwork on either side of its nose, with a white and purple orchid adorning the lower left cowling and the name *Rita* applied in white script on the lower right cowling. DeHaven later flew two other P-40Ns before eventually converting to the P-38 in the autumn of 1944, and he used the Lockheed fighter to increase his score to 14 confirmed victories.

18

P-38L-5 (serial unknown) of Capt Bob DeHaven, 7th FS/49th FG, Tacloban (Leyte), November 1944

7th FS Ops Executive Bob DeHaven was another veteran V Fighter Command ace who enjoyed himself in the target rich skies over Leyte in the autumn of 1944. He claimed four kills and one damaged between 29 October and 4 November, and all of these victories were almost certainly achieved in this P-38L-5. Quite possibly one of the ex-8th or 475th FG Lightnings hastily commandeered as attrition replacements by the 49th FG in early November, this aircraft was marked with the appropriate blue squadron colours of the 7th FS. And although the fighter did not feature either DeHaven's name or scoreboard beneath the cockpit, someone had still found the time to adorn its twin fins with the 'Screamin' Demons'' Bunyip emblem synonymous with the 7th FS during its spell in Darwin defending northern Australia in 1942. Also featured on the cover of this volume, DeHaven's P-38L-5 was reportedly destroyed in an enemy bombing raid soon after its pilot returned home on leave in mid November.

19

P-47D (serial unknown) of Capt Wally Jordan, CO of the 9th FS/49th FG, Gusap, March 1944

Wally Jordan was one of just a handful of 9th FS pilots to claim a victory with the P-47, the unit CO downing an 'Oscar' on 14 March 1944. This doubled his score, for he had destroyed a Ki-43 on 2 August 1943 whilst flying a P-38H-1. Jordan had taken over command of the 9th when 'Jerry' Johnson was sent home on leave on 29 January 1944. As with Johnson's Thunderbolt, Jordan had his machine marked with command stripes mid fuselage.

20

P-38L-5 (serial unknown) of Maj Wally Jordan, 49th FG HQ, Biak, October 1944

By the time Wally Jordan was issued with this aircraft in late October 1944, he had claimed all six of his kills – three of these had come earlier that same month in a P-38L-1. Although a member of the 49th FG HQ flight, he kept his aircraft 'stabled' with his old unit, the 9th FS, hence its red spinners. Also note the fighter's 49th FG staff stripes forward of the twin fins. With the coming of the Philippines invasion, pre-war Army Air Corps tri-colour rudder markings were adopted by several USAAF groups, including the 49th FG.

21

P-47D-16 42-76059 of Maj Ed Roddy, 58th FG HQ, Saidor, June 1944

One of the least publicised fighter groups in the SWPA, the 58th FG spent much of its war pounding Japanese targets on the ground. Indeed, the group scored just 14 confirmed kills during the entire Pacific War. Ed Roddy was already an ace when he was posted to the 58th FG from the 348th FG in February 1944. Made group operations officer, he was issued with this command-striped P-47D-16 soon after joining the 58th, and it remained his mount well into the summer.

22

P-47D-2 42-8096 of Lt Col Dick Rowland, CO of the 348th FG, Port Moresby, November 1943

Dick Rowland claimed at least two of his first five kills in this P-47D-2, which was also his original *Miss Mutt*. Aside from this titling, the Thunderbolt also featured female nose art and the inscription *PRIDE OF LODI OHIO* (Rowland's home town) just forward of the fuselage star and bar. Despite the aircraft's heavy usage in harsh tropical conditions, it was kept in immaculate condition by its hardworking groundcrew.

23

P-47D-4 42-22684 of Lt Col Dick Rowland, CO of the 348th FG, Finschhafen, late December 1943

This aircraft was issued to the 348th FG CO as a replacement for battle-weary D-2 42-8096 in late November 1943, and like its predecessor, it was flown devoid of command stripes. These do not appear to have been adopted by the 348th FG at any stage of the SWPA campaign.

24

P-51D-15 44-15103 of Col Dick Rowland, CO of the 348th FG, San Marcelino (Luzon), early 1945

P-51D-15 44-15103 was Col Rowland's final mount during his long tour of duty in command of the 348th FG. Always one for unique personal markings on his various aircraft, he had the fighter adorned with a map of Ohio, complete with two stars – the top one was for his home town of Lodi, but the significance of the location of the second star remains a mystery. Rowland abandoned the *Miss Mutt* nickname when his group switched from Thunderbolts to Mustangs, christening his fighters *DIRTY DICK* instead. 44-15103 was the last machine to bear this sobriquet.

25

P-47D-2 42-22532 of Maj Bill Banks, CO of the 342nd FS/ 348th FG, Finschhafen, February 1944

Providing a sober contrast in colours and markings to the late war P-47s flown by the 348th FG, this aircraft was almost certainly used by Bill Banks to down some, if not all, of his five kills in New Guinea in the final four months of 1943. However, he did not use it to claim his sixth kill on 7 February 1944, despite the victory symbol appearing on 42-22532. By then Banks had been issued with a newer P-47D-3, although he appears to have flown the two fighters concurrently for a short while.

26

P-51K-10 44-12073 of Lt Col Bill Banks, CO of the 348th FG, Ie Shima, July 1945

One of the most strikingly marked of all Pacific fighters, *SUNSHINE VII* was flown by 348th FG Col Bill Banks from Ie Shima during the final months of the war in the Pacific. Colourful stripes on the spinner and through the fighter's nickname denoted the four squadrons within the group – the 348th FG was the only group in V Fighter Command to control four units. Such markings on the propeller spinner were standard practice for the group CO's machine at this stage of the war, the colours denoting the 460th (black), 342nd (blue), 341st (yellow) and 340th (red) FSs.

27

P-47D-4 42-22694 of 1Lt Marvin Grant, 342nd FS/ 348th FG, Finschhafen, late December 1943

Returning to the subdued colours and markings of the 348th FG's New Guinea period, this P-47D-4 was the mount of seven-kill ace Marvin Grant for a number of months in 1943-44. He had claimed two kills in his previous P-47D-2 just a matter of days prior to replacing it with this machine in late December 1943. Note the P-47's unpainted windscreen framing and blue tail stripe, the latter denoting the fighter's assignment to the 342nd FS.

28

P-47D-23 42-27886 of Capt Marvin Grant, 342nd FS/ 348th FG, Leyte, November 1944

This unusually marked P-47D-23 features victory symbols for all seven of Grant's kills, although he failed to claim any of these with this particular machine. He did, however use the immaculate Thunderbolt to attack Japanese troops on a near-daily basis during the bitterly fought campaign to retake the Philippines. The red, blue and white striping along the length of the fuselage was an identification marking introduced by the 342nd FS in late 1944.

29

P-47D-23 42-27884 of Maj Bill Dunham, CO of the 460th FS/348th FG, Leyte, December 1944

Undoubtedly the 348th FG's most colourful Thunderbolt, P-47D-23 42-27884 *Bonnie* was the mount of 460th FS CO Maj Bill Dunham for much of the group's campaign in the Philippines. And it was definitely more than just a 'show pony', for Dunham used it to claim five kills in two missions on 7 and 14 December 1944.

30

P-51K-10 44-12017 of Lt Col Bill Dunham, Deputy CO of the 348th FG, Ie Shima, August 1945

P-51K-10 44-12017 *"MRS. BONNIE"* was the final wartime fighter assigned to Bill Dunham in the Pacific, the aircraft being issued to him at around the same time as he was promoted to lieutenant colonel and made deputy CO of the 348th FG. Dunham used it to claim his last kill (a Ki-84 'Frank) on 1 August 1945.

31

P-38J-15 42-104024 of Col Charles MacDonald, CO of the 475th FG, Hollandia, May 1944

This aircraft was Col MacDonald's first natural metal P-38, being delivered to the 475th FG in February 1944. The fighter was maintained by the 433rd FS during its time with the group, squadron records indicating that it remained on charge until August 1944. Japanese aircraft were rarely seen in the skies over New Guinea in the summer of that year, and MacDonald claimed just three aircraft destroyed and 1.5 damaged during this period. Some reports unofficially claim that this machine was lost in a landing accident soon after MacDonald was ordered home on enforced leave on 4 August as punishment for letting legendary civilian pilot Charles Lindbergh see combat during his time 'advising' the 475th FG in June-July 1944.

32

P-38H-1 42-66682 of Capt John Loisel, CO of the 432nd FS/475th FG, Dobodura, late January 1944

Loisel claimed as many as four of his eleven kills in this aircraft, which he christened *SCREAMIN' KID*. P-38s would typically survive less than six months in the frontline with V Fighter Command, but 42-66682 remained in service with the 475th FG for more than eight. Indeed, Loisel claimed his first kills with it as early as 15 October 1943 when he downed two 'Zekes' over Oro Bay. He continued to fly the aircraft on and off until late January 1944, when the first of the vastly improved J-models arrived in the Solomons.

33

P-38L-5 44-25643 of Maj John Loisel, 475th FG HQ, Dulag (Leyte), late January 1945

This aircraft was originally assigned to Col MacDonald, who marked it up as 'blue 100' *PUTT PUTT MARU*. Group records indicate that it was issued to the group CO as a replacement for 44-24843, which was lost in combat on 2 January. Inexplicably passed on to 475th FG Ops Officer Maj Loisel later that same month, 44-25643 (minus its distinctive nose art, and with its side number changed to 'yellow 101') is listed as having been badly damaged in a taxiing accident on 27 January. The incident occurred at Dulag in wet conditions when the 432nd FS's Lt Arnold Larsen landed 'hot and flat' and skidded into the stationary Loisel, who had just led a four-ship patrol back to base. Both fighters were despatched to the 10th Service Squadron for repairs to be affected, and 44-25643 later returned to action with the 8th FG's 80th FS.

34

P-38H-5 42-66817 of Capt Tom McGuire, 431st FS/475th FG, Dobodura, late December 1943

This particular P-38H-5 was McGuire's second Lightning, his first (H-1 42-66592) having been written off following damaged inflicted by enemy cannon fire during a dogfight near Wewak on 29 August 1943 – its pilot claimed a 'Zeke' and a 'Tony' destroyed in return. 42-66817 lasted until it was replaced by a new J-model in late January 1944, McGuire having by then raised his tally to 16 confirmed kills (few of these were scored in this particular machine, however).

35

P-38L-1 44-24155 of Maj Tom McGuire, CO of the 431st FS/475th FG, Dulag (Leyte), early November 1944

McGuire's most successful P-38 was undoubtedly *PUDGY (V)*, alias 44-24155, which he flew from late October through to early January 1945, when the Lightning was removed from the frontline and sent to a servicing unit for overhaul. By then McGuire had claimed at least 14 kills with it, taking his final tally to 38 victories. It is depicted here after he had claimed his first success (a Ki-44 'Tojo') with the fighter, on 1 November 1944. *PUDGY (V)* was sat at Dulag awaiting despatch to a servicing unit when McGuire sortied for the last time (in 431st FS P-38L-1 44-24845) on 7 January 1945.

36

P-38L-5 44-25600 of Maj Elliot Summer, CO of the 432nd FS/475th FG, Lingayen (Luzon), July 1945

This aircraft was the final mount of ten-kill ace Elliot Summer, although by the time it was issued to him in early 1945 he had claimed all of his aerial victories. The fighter was unusual in that it boasted the 432nd FS's emblem on its nose, along with the more standard CO's stripes and yellow unit markings. 'Yellow 140' was always the number assigned to the squadron commander's aircraft, and 44-25600's brief reign as the CO's mount ended when Summer rotated back home in July 1945. Just a matter of days later, on the 20th of that same month, the fighter was lost on a training flight when its pilot, Lt Frazee, suffered complete electrical failure and was forced to bale out.

BIBLIOGRAPHY

Boyce, Col J Ward (editor), *American Fighter Aces Album.* The American Fighter Aces Association, 1996

Ferguson, S W and Pascalis William K, *Protect & Avenge - the 49th Fighter Group in World War II.* Schiffer, 1996

Hess, William N, *Pacific Sweep.* Doubleday, 1974

Maloney, Edward T (editor), *Fighter Tactics of the Aces S.W.P.A.* World War II Publications, 1978

Molesworth, Carl, *Osprey Aircraft of the Aces 55 - P-40 Warhawk Aces of the Pacific.* Osprey, 2003

O'Leary, Michael, *Production Line to Frontline 3 - Lockheed P-38 Lightning.* Osprey, 1999

O'Leary, Michael, *USAAF Fighters of World War 2.* Blandford Press, 1986

Olynyk, Frank, *Stars & Bars - A Tribute to the American Fighter Ace 1920-1973.* Grub Street, 1995

Stanaway, John C and Hickey Larry, *Attack & Conquer - The 8th Fighter Group in World War II.* Schiffer, 1995

Stanaway, John C, *Kearby's Thunderbolts - The 348th Fighter Group in World War II.* Schiffer, 1997

Stanaway, John C, *Possum, Clover & Hades - The 475th Fighter Group in World War II.* Schiffer, 1993

Stanaway, John, *Kearby's Thunderbolts - The 348th Fighter Group in World War II.* Phalanx, 1992

Stanaway, John, *Peter Three Eight - The Pilots' Story.* Pictorial Histories Publishing Company, 1986

Stanaway, John, *Kearby's Thunderbolts - The 348th Fighter Group in World War II.* Phalanx, 1992

Stanaway, John, *Osprey Aircraft of the Aces 14 - P-38 Lightning Aces of the Pacific and CBI.* Osprey, 1997

Stanaway, John, *Osprey Aircraft of the Aces 26 - Mustang and Thunderbolt Aces of the Pacific and CBI.* Osprey, 1999

Toliver, Raymond F and Constable Trevor J, *Fighter Aces of the USA.* Schiffer, 1997

INDEX

References to illustrations are shown in **bold**. Plates are shown with page and caption locators in brackets.